the book of Vodou

The Book of Vodou

Charms and rituals to empower your life

Leah Gordon

A QUARTO BOOK

All inquiries should be addressed to:
Barron's Educational Series, Inc.
250 Wireless Boulevard
Hauppauge, NY 11788
http://www.barronseduc.com

Library of Congress Catalog Card Number: 99-69859

International Standard Book Number: 0-7641-5249-1

Conceived, designed, and produced by
Quarto Publishing plc
The Old Brewery
6 Blundell Street
London N7 9BH

QUAR: KEJW

Editor: *Michelle Pickering*
Art editor: *Rebecca Adams*
Designers: *Rebecca Adams & Mabel Chan*
Assistant art director: *Penny Cobb*
Photographer: *Rosa Rodrigo*
Illustrator: *Sarah Adams*
Picture researcher: *Laurent Boubounelle*
Indexer: *Dorothy Frame*

Art director: *Moira Clinch*
Publisher: *Piers Spence*

Manufactured by Regent Publishing Services Ltd,
Hong Kong
Printed by Midas Printing Ltd, China

9 8 7 6 5 4 3 2 1

author's note

This book contains information
for authentic Vodou charms.
The author would like to stress
that these charms should be
administered or monitored by
a Vodou priest or priestess, using
the authentic Haitian ingredients
rather than alternatives, if they
are to be effective.

Contents

Vodou is a fascinating religion. It was born in west and central Africa, and traveled on the transatlantic slave ships to the New World, where it flourished in Haiti, on the island of Hispaniola. Vodou is characterized by ceremony, music, dance, and sacrifice, through which participants commune with the spirits of their ancestors via divine possession.

Introduction

Vodou has a pantheon of spirits, called *lwa*, whose power can be invoked in a variety of ways. The various spirits reign over different areas of life, from love to wealth and from health to family. Each spirit has its own identity, symbols, ritualistic objects, songs, and dances. For centuries, Vodou has been the victim of fear, superstition, and ignorance—the very crimes of which Vodou itself has been accused. This book is a matter-of-fact and engaging introduction to this much-maligned religion, providing a guide to the spirits and their symbols, and describing some of the intricate ceremonies, charms, and rituals that make up the practice of Vodou.

The spelling of Vodou

The spelling Vodou has been used throughout this book, rather than the more well-known voodoo. This is part of a process of acknowledgment and acceptance of the Vodou religion. Vodou is the *Kreyòl* (Creole) spelling for the religion, and is used by its adherents in Haiti. The spelling Vodou is now increasingly being used outside Haiti in an attempt to differentiate the practice of the religion from the perceived "mumbo jumbo" that the spelling voodoo conjures. There are many other *Kreyòl* words and spellings in this book, which are presented in italics. Haitians exist on a symbiotic mix of French and *Kreyòl* spellings, but for the sake of consistency we have adhered to *Kreyòl* spellings throughout the text.

Drummers and ounsi (singers and dancers) taking part in a Vodou ceremony in Haiti's capital city, Port-au-Prince. Music and dancing are used to coax the spirits from their divine homeland to the mortal world.

Vodou is a deeply spiritual and visually dazzling religion, encompassing intricate rituals, song, and dance. This chapter examines the development of Vodou in Haiti, from its roots in Africa to the crucial role it played in Haitian history—the first country where slaves overthrew their colonial masters and achieved independence. The intricacies of Vodou ceremonies are explored, the religion's sacred symbols explained, and its unique art forms displayed.

inside VODOU

When Columbus first discovered the island of Hispaniola, in 1492, it was inhabited by the Taino Indians of the Arawak tribe. It is estimated that 400,000 indigenous Indians inhabited the island when the Spanish landed. The Tainos lived in permanent villages, containing mud and thatch huts that were grouped around a main square. They had a deeply instilled sense of tribal unity and justice, and lived in relative peace and harmony. They also practiced a skillful form of land conservation, never using slash and burn, but instead replenishing the soil with compost. The Tainos had their own religious beliefs, based around two supreme gods, Yúcahu and Atabey, and a host of lesser spirits who inhabited trees, streams, and inanimate objects.

the history of Haiti

Enslavement

The peaceful Tainos were soon enslaved by the Spanish invaders and set to work in gold mines. After 30 years of slavery, fewer than a thousand Tainos were left alive on the island—from an estimated original number of 400,000. Those not worked to death took their own lives in order to escape the abject misery of their lives as slaves. Some of them escaped into the mountains to live in secret encampments, and are thought to have cohabited briefly with runaway African slaves, who were brought to Hispaniola at the beginning of the 16th century to replace the Tainos as a labor force. Vestiges of Taino culture can still be found in Haiti today, in the sound of the conch shell horn, woven into the patterns of Vodou *veve*, and in the use of magical stones.

By the mid-16th century, over 20,000 black slaves had been shipped from Africa to Hispaniola. In 1697, the island was divided by the Treaty of Ryswick and the French took control of the western third of Hispaniola, calling it Saint-Domingue. The French continued the import of African slaves to work in their newly founded sugar plantations. By 1790, the number of African slaves in Saint-Domingue had reached at least half a million. The colony became one of the richest in the Caribbean, paid for by the sweat and blood of the African slaves.

Engraving showing African villagers being taken as slaves, and the cramped conditions they endured on board the slave ships on the long journey to Saint-Domingue.

Independence

On arrival in Saint-Domingue, the French were always careful to divide members of the same tribe, and therefore split groups of slaves who spoke the same language, in order to avoid dissent. Religious ritual became the sole arena within which the slaves could find common ground and solidarity. Vodou was practiced in secret on the plantations and thrived among the maroons, the runaway slaves who set up camps in the inhospitable mountains of the island. By the late 18th century, dissent among the slaves was rife, fueled by stories of the French Revolution. In 1791, the dissent came to a head and turned into rebellion, and a 13-year struggle between the French and the blacks ensued.

Vodou was both the inspiration and precipitation of the long fight for Haiti's independence. On August 14th, 1791, during a violent storm, a Vodou priest called Boukman performed a ceremony in a woodland clearing called Bois Cayman. Slaves and maroons gathered from all over the region. Illuminated by lightning, Boukman sacrificed a black pig for the African ancestors and in its blood wrote the words "liberty or death." Inspired and invigorated, the slaves returned to their plantations and spread the message of rebellion. Within days the fertile plains were set on fire, burning with a passion for freedom that did not dampen until independence in 1804. Saint-Domingue became the first black republic in the New World and was renamed Haiti, the original Taino name for the country, whose meaning is mountainous land. (What is now the Dominican Republic was established in the remaining two-thirds of the island and declared its independence in 1844.)

Engraving showing the revolt of the slaves in Saint-Domingue in 1791.

Jean-Jacques Dessalines, who led Haiti to independence and crowned himself emperor. Born a slave, he quickly proved to have great tactical talents as a leader of the rebellion.

Religious roots

The Vodou religion originates from the animist beliefs of 14th-century Africa. It is a synthesis of many West and Central African religious practices, crossed with residual Taino beliefs and ornamented with Catholicism. For a number of complex reasons, and in part to humor the Christian missionaries while retaining their own belief system, the slaves incorporated icons of the Catholic saints onto their altars, secretly using them to represent various Vodou spirits. Vodou is split into different "nations," each of which is made up of a different assembly of *lwa*, or spirits. The two principal nations are Rada and Petwo. The Rada spirits are considered "cooler," gentler, and more conciliatory than the Petwo spirits, who are "hotter," more quick-tempered, and fiery.

Danbala, a "cool" spirit of the Rada nation.

The three-horned Bosou, a "hot" spirit of the Petwo nation.

13

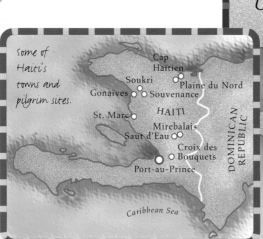

some of
Haiti's
towns and
pilgrim sites.

Cap
Haïtien

Soukri
Gonaïves   Souvenance

Plaine du Nord

St. Marc

HAITI

Mirebalais
Saut d'Eau

DOMINICAN REPUBLIC

Croix des
Bouquets

Port-au-Prince

Caribbean Sea

U.S.A.

CUBA

HAITI

SOUTH
AMERICA

African origins

Some of the tribal peoples from whom
Africans were taken as slaves include:

The Senegalese, Foule, and Mandingue
tribes from the Fula and Mandingo
empires.

The Agoua and Caplaou tribes from the
Ashanti and Fanti empires.

The Rada and Adja tribes from the
Dahomey empire.

The Fon, Ibo, and Nago tribes from the
Hausa, Benin, and Yoruba empires.

The Kongo tribe from the Kongo empire.

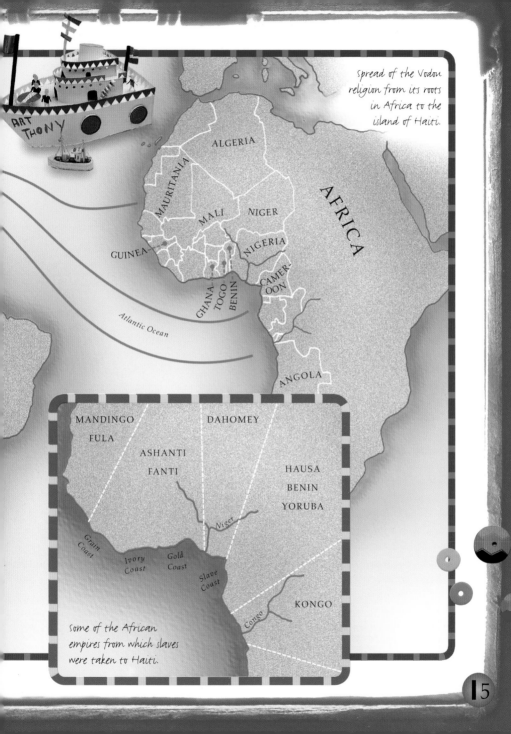

spread of the Vodou
religion from its roots
in Africa to the
island of Haiti.

ART THONY

ALGERIA

MAURITANIA

MALI

NIGER

AFRICA

GUINEA-

NIGERIA

GHANA-
TOGO-
BENIN

CAMER-
OON

Atlantic Ocean

ANGOLA

MANDINGO

DAHOMEY

FULA

ASHANTI

FANTI

HAUSA

BENIN

YORUBA

Niger

Grain
Coast

Ivory
Coast

Gold
Coast

Slave
Coast

KONGO

Congo

some of the African
empires from which slaves
were taken to Haiti.

Sorcery

Vodouists perceive the universe as a magical cosmos, in which man is born of magic and all men are potential magicians. Sorcery is considered to be magic utilized for bad intent, and the manipulation of spiritual forces for personal gain. Those who embrace Vodou acknowledge sorcery but do not necessarily practice it. Many are quick to disassociate themselves from any connection with it.

The work of the red sects

Stories of sorcery are part of the folkloric heritage of Haiti, and embedded deep within the collective psyche. Some of the spirits, often from the Petwo nation, engage themselves with sorcery, including Kriminèl and the three-horned Bosou. There are supposed to be many secret societies that practice sorcery along similar lines to the societies of Freemasonry. These "red sects" are called *zobob, bizango, vlenblendeng,* and *makandel,* depending on the region.

A *bòkò,* or sorcerer, is an individual who perverts the forces of the magical universe. He is said, pejoratively, to "work with the left hand," or if he is also a Vodou priest, to "serve with both hands." The sorcerer carries out his works at a crossroads or in a cemetery. The most feared act a sorcerer can undertake is *voye lamò,* meaning to send death, which is done under the auspices of St. Expedit. Under such a curse, the victim is supposed to wither, vomit blood, and die. Sorcerers also make *wanga,* which is an object, package, or poison that can harm or bring misfortune to other people. The sorcerer creates these poisons from herbs and

Sorcerers use secret combinations of different herbs and powders to induce illness and fear in their victims.

powders using secret recipes, and it is thought that just one pinch can bring bad luck or illness.

Zombification

Another sorcerous practice is the creation of *zombi*. These are people who appear to have died and have been interred. They are then dug up and brought back to life some days later. Once resurrected, their will ceases to be their own, and they submit to the commands of their owner in a stupor of idiocy. It is believed that the sorcerer concocts a poison from different animal and vegetable sources, and administers this to the unfortunate victim. The poison induces a coma that is indistinguishable from death, because the breathing is so light as to be negligible. Then when the bogus corpse is dug up, an antidote is administered that appears to bring the body back to life.

When people die in suspicious circumstances in Haiti, the corpse is often shot or strangled to save it from a life of enslavement as a *zombi*. The fear of enslavement is at the heart of the *zombi* mythology. During the struggle for independence, the Haitian slaves vowed that they would choose death rather than a return to slavery, and the *zombi* represents their deepest fear.

Papier maché statue of the Petwo spirit Kriminèl, by Jean Romy Jean Louis.

Nurturing the divinities through long and elaborate ceremonies is one of the central aspects of Vodou practice. There are endless variations within ceremonial observance, depending on the purpose of the ritual and the spirit being honored. The celebrants use a fusion of drumming, singing, and dancing to coax the spirit to the mortal world to be fed and invigorated by the gift of sacrifice.

Vodou
Ceremonies

Greeting the spirits

The *ounfò*, the Vodou temple, comprises a communal space—the *peristil*—at the center of which is the sacred post—the *poto mitan*—around which the ceremonies revolve. Surrounding the *peristil* are smaller side rooms known as *badji*, which are the altar rooms that house the divine and ritualistic objects. A typical Rada ceremony, to feed the spirits, begins with liturgical prayer, drumming, and song. Each spirit responds to its own particular melodies, lyrics, and rhythms. During a ceremony, the *oungan* (priest) or *manbo* (priestess) salutes and greets many of the spirits from the eternal pantheon. Carrying the *ason*, the sacred rattle, from the altar, the priest must first greet Papa Legba, the spirit of the crossroads,

and request that he open the gates to the domain of the divine. The four cardinal points are saluted with a respectful bow and a shake of the rattle. After this, the priest greets the Marasa, the divine twins, and Loko Atisou, the spirit of the original priest.

Next, the *laplas*, the master of the sword, enters the *peristil* from the *badji*, flanked by the two *rèn drapo*, the flag queens, who carry the ceremonial sequinned flags. The priest kisses the hilt of the sword and the poles of the flags as the four cardinal points are again saluted. Using cornmeal from a rough gourd vessel, the priest traces the

A priest shaking the ason, the sacred rattle, at the base of the poto mitan during a ceremony in Port-au-Prince.

veve, the sacred symbol, for Ayizan, the spirit of the first priestess, on the floor of the *peristil*. While this is in progress, the *ounsi* (singers and dancers) shred palm leaves. Honor and respect has now been paid to the powerful cosmic spirits who preside over the ceremony and rarely appear through possession.

Ceremonial possession

The congregation now greets the other Vodou spirits, who herald their presence through possession. Possession is the supreme blessing that the spirits can bestow upon the celebrants. It is seen as proof that the divine hunger has been satiated. During possession, the *lwa* mount the celebrants as a rider mounts a horse. With the divine bit between their teeth, the celebrants take on the mannerisms and characteristics of the sacred horsemen. It is possible to discern the nature of the possessing spirit through the movements and actions of the meta-physically engulfed mortal.

First, the congregation greets Danbala, the snake spirit, who forces the possessed celebrant to writhe and undulate on the temple floor.

A food offering of popcorn and
the blood of a sacrificial animal for
Ezili Dantò, which has been placed on
top of her veve, drawn in cornmeal.

The drumbeats change again, assuming a faster pace and more insistent beat, to greet more Rada spirits, including Ezili Freda, the *lwa* of love, and Agwe, the master of the oceans. As the atmosphere heats up, Ogou will arrive, wearing a red scarf, carrying a sword, and drinking rum. After all the other spirits have appeared, Gede, the spirit of the graveyard, will impose his bawdy, lewd, and sexual disposition on the congregation, challenging and mocking the assembly.

After possession, the celebrant is exhausted but unharmed, and has no memory of the event. Possession is the ultimate accolade of Vodou faith, granting consummate communion with the spirits, not unlike the mystical exaltations of the enraptured Christian saints.

Blood sacrifice

After the spirits have been honored and greeted, beasts are sacrificed and offerings laid out to satiate and replenish the spirits. The blood sacrifice is the climax of the ceremony, and each spirit has a favorite animal. The sacrificial animals are arduously prepared before the ceremony with baths, perfumes, and powders, and feast upon divine foods before the holy execution. After death, the animals' blood is collected in a gourd and mixed with salt, syrup, and rum and often smeared on the lips of the *ounsi* by the priest. The body of the victim is decorated with cornmeal *veve*, showered with money offerings, and finally cooked to be shared between the spirits and the congregation.

Symbolic items are kept in the temple and worn when honoring particular spirits. For example, a straw hat is worn to honor the peasant spirit Papa Zaka.

Tools of the trade

The *oungan* (priest) or *manbo* (priestess) holds authority over those who have initiated within his or her temple, and is said to have the invisible knowledge, which brings spiritual insight and the ability to channel divine forces. Instruction into the priesthood can take many years. The priest or priestess must pass through the many ranks of Vodou: from initiate to *oungenikon*, the leader of the chorus, to *laplas*, the master of the sword, and to *konfyans*, the assistant to the priest or priestess, before finally "taking the *ason*" and achieving priestly status. He or she must manage a temple, furnish the altars, and organize and officiate the many ceremonies held for the spirits.

Small wicker chairs are useful for exhausted celebrants who need a short post-possession rest. They are also needed for the *ounsi* to sit on while tending fires during special ceremonies.

The priest must keep many different colored scarves in the temple to be worn in honor of the various spirits.

Strings of ceremonial beads are worn, crossed over the chest, during initiation ceremonies.

A priest always has a deck of playing cards at hand in order to perform divination.

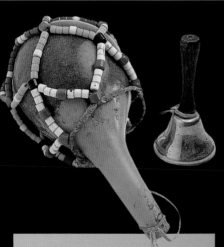

The *ason* is a ritual rattle used for both summoning and soothing the spirits. It is made from a gourd containing snake vertebrae, and covered in a lattice of colored beads with a small bell attached.

A sharpened dagger must be kept in the temple for performing animal sacrifice at the climax of the ceremony.

Every participant has a role to play in Vodou ceremonies, including singing, drumming, and dancing. These form an interlinked troika of aural and visual invitations that charm the spirits to earth. The congregants collectively create a musical drama, a cacophony of praise, in order to magnetize the spirits toward the mortal world.

Music and Dance

Singing

The singing is called *chante lwa*, and is a choral invitation to the spirits, imploring them to join the congregation and feast on the offerings. The Vodou chorus uses call and response between the song leader, the *ounjenikon*, and the choir. The role of the *ounjenikon* is paramount, as he or she is the sonic soul of the congregation, divining which songs will best draw and praise the *lwa*. Most of the songs are in *Kreyòl*, but there are some words of *langaj*, an ancient African language whose exact meaning has been lost in the mists of time. Each spirit has its own unique array of special songs and must be offered three or seven songs performed in a predetermined order.

Drumming

The drums are the primary musical instrument within Vodou worship. Celebrants often refer to ceremonies as *bat tambou*, which means beating the drums. Even though the drummers themselves are secular, often uninitiated and employed purely as musicians, the drums are sacred instruments and must be baptized before use

A boula drum, the smallest of the Rada trinity of drums (left); a maraca used by Rara street bands (top).

Drummers during
a ceremony in
Carrefour Feuilles,
Port-au-Prince.

during a ceremony. The rhythms of the drums are used to call and energize the spirits of Africa and Ginen, the divine homeland of the ancestors.

A skillful drummer can concentrate the vigor of the dancers and contribute to the trancelike quality of the ceremonies. The drummer needs to learn a vast number of diverse rhythms to court the various spirits, and to have remarkable energy and stamina to play out a whole ceremony.

Each nation of spirits has different types of drums and their own unique rhythms. Within the Rada nation, for example, there are three drums: the *manman*, the principal drum; the *segon*, the second, medium-sized drum; and the *boula*, the smallest drum. The body of a Rada drum is carved from the trunk of a tree; a goatskin is then stretched over the top, and secured using wooden pegs and cords, to make the head. The three drums are always played in conjunction with each other. The *manman* is played with the hand and a small wooden hammer, using both the rim and the drumhead; the *segon* is played with the hand and a forked stick; and the *boula* is played with two long sticks. There is

Ounsi singing and dancing during a ceremony in Bel Air, Port-au-Prince.

a fourth musician who uses an iron rod to strike a metal plate or bell, called an *ogan*, and keeps the pace throughout the ceremony.

The drums must be invigorated from time to time during special ceremonies called *kouche tambou*, putting the drums to bed, and *ba tambou mange*, feeding the drums. The drums are laid in the *badji*, a ritual altar room in the Vodou temple, on a bed of banana leaves. A candle is lit on each drum, and ritual food and drink sprinkled over the instruments of the divine to feed and energize them. A machete is driven into the ground in front of the drums and a white sheet is hung over them. They are

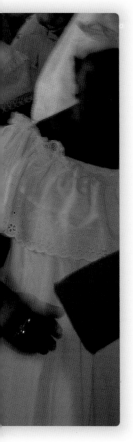

left like this for a night while the spirits of the wood cross the sacred water to the ancestral homeland and replenish their power.

Dancing

Dance, along with song and drumbeat, is the third element of the ritual triumvirate used to call and charm the spirits. The dancers, known as *ounsi*, attract the *lwa*, and in turn the *lwa* infect the dancers by possession. The dancers are then compelled to dance to a metaphysical beat, often with a passion and panache that they did not possess earlier. The *ounsi* perform different dances to honor individual spirits. Sometimes during a chorus for Agwe, the dancers' bodies flow like fish under the waves, and while honoring Danbala, they undulate sinuously like serpents. The women often hold the hems of their dresses during the dance, while male dancers hold either end of a scarf draped around their necks.

The dances, as with the drumming and the songs, differ according to the nation of spirits being honored.

The most complex, intricate, and passionate dances are those of the Kongo nation of spirits. The dancing during a ceremony is vibrant and lively and may appear to be chaotic, but there is an underlying pattern and order that is aided by the agility and virtuosity of the dancers.

A cornet used by Rara street bands during carnival season in Haiti.

Although the most potent portrayal of the spirits is through the act of possession, there are also many material representations of the divine. These objects are kept on the altars of the relevant spirits, and used within the ceremony to symbolize the spirits.

the Symbols
of Vodou

Ritualistic objects

These objects have no inherent special powers, but they act as physical reminders of the divinity and as accessories for a celebrant possessed by the relevant spirit. For example, a sword signifies Ogou, the warrior spirit; a cross symbolizes Gede, spirit of the cemeteries. Ezili Freda, in particular, has a plethora of symbolic objects due to her materialistic nature. Her altar must contain combs, brushes, jewelry, soaps, perfumes, flowers, and a special baby blue dress. Each spirit is also symbolized by a particular color. Scarves of the colors sacred to the lwa are kept in the *badji*, the altar rooms, and used to mop the celebrants' brows during possession. Sequinned flags, bearing elaborate designs symbolic of a particular spirit, are used to herald the start of the ceremony.

Catholic counterparts

Each spirit has a Catholic saint with whom it is identified. These saintly counterparts originate from the era of slavery and the enforcement of Christianity upon the African slaves. The slaves subverted the meanings of the saints by adopting them as icons of their own African gods. Small details in the visual iconography of the saints

A crude metal cross from an altar for Gede (above); scarves made in a spirit's associated color are kept on the spirit's altar (left).

became signifiers for characteristics of their own spirits. Thus, St. Gerard is syncretic with Gede as he is seated next to a skull and lilies, symbols of death; St. Jacques represents Ogou, the warrior spirit, because of the sword he brandishes; and St. Patrick is symbolic of Danbala, due to the snakes at his feet.

Each Vodou spirit is identified with a Catholic saint. St. Cosmas and St. Damian symbolize the Marasa, the sacred twins.

The poto mitan

The most powerful symbol in the temple is the *poto mitan*, the sacred post located in the center of the *peristil* and around which all the ceremonies revolve. It reaches from the ceiling to the floor, from the divine to the mortal, from heaven to earth. The *poto mitan*

Chromolithographs of the Virgin Mary are placed on altars for Ezili Freda, the spirit of love and beauty.

A pair of makout and a denim jacket, hanging alongside a priest's ason and above a picture of a saint, in a Vodou temple in Haiti. They are worn during the ceremony to honor Papa Zaka.

Painting by Rose-Marie Desruisseaux showing the ounsi (singers and dancers) dancing around the poto mitan during a Vodou ceremony. The poto mitan is the cosmic axis of the temple and provides a passageway through which the divinities can enter the mortal world.

symbolizes the highway of the *lwa*, and acts as a sacred lightning conductor transporting the current of divine energy to the temple. The post is set into a circular stone plinth that is usually about 1 foot (30 cm) high. The plinth serves as an altar during ceremonies, where offerings are left and libations poured. The *poto mitan* is decorated with spiraling designs that represent Danbala.

Priest drawing a cornmeal veve during a ceremony in Bel Air, Port-au-Prince.

Symbolic veve

Each spirit has its own symbolic drawing, a *veve*, which is traced on the ground during the ceremony using cornmeal, wood ash, powdered red brick, or, sometimes, even gunpowder. The powder is held in a half calabash shell and trickled from the fingers to produce the thin lines of the elaborate design. The process is very skillful, as the patterns created are geometrically complex and intricate. The drawing of the *veve* is an arresting and theatrical aspect of any Vodou ceremony. Some *veve* are drawn singly, for an individual spirit, while others may be interlinked, spanning the length of the temple and honoring a host of spirits.

Once the *veve* has been traced, it is sprinkled with libations of rum and small offerings of food are laid upon it. The priest or priestess then shakes the *ason*—the sacred rattle—over the *veve*,

muttering prayers, and places a lit candle in the center. The purpose of the *veve* is to summon and focus the *lwa*. While music and dance charm and attract the *lwa*, the *veve* perform more potent magic, and oblige the spirits to manifest themselves. They are an irresistible magnet for divine attention.

The *veve* have diverse cultural roots, spanning the passage from Africa to Haiti. Primarily they originate from the animist religious practices of Dahomey, but the patterns have been influenced by French filigree ironwork designs as well as the symbols of the indigenous Taino Indians of Haiti. There are also vestiges of Freemasonry in the symbols depicted on the *veve* and Vodou flags, including stars, a builder's compass, picks, spades, and coffins.

the **V**eve

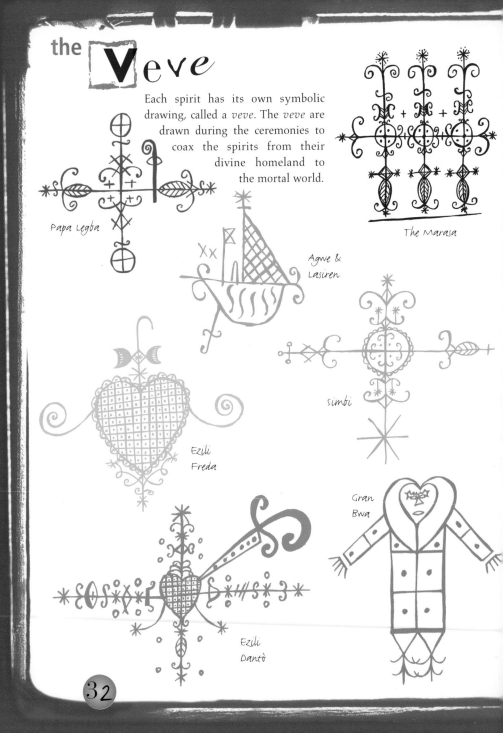

Each spirit has its own symbolic drawing, called a *veve*. The *veve* are drawn during the ceremonies to coax the spirits from their divine homeland to the mortal world.

Papa Legba

The Marasa

Agwe & Lasiren

Simbi

Ezili Freda

Gran Bwa

Ezili Dantò

32

Loko Atisou

Ayizan

Danbala & Ayida Wèdo

Papa Zaka

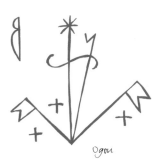

Ogou

Bosou

Gede

The sacred altar rooms of the Vodou temple are used to store and display a plethora of objects in honor of the spirits. In addition to the symbolic objects associated with the particular spirit during possession, other items, such as bottles, dolls, and *paket kongo*, are also kept there.

bottles, DoLLs, and paket kongo

A doll's head in a bottle used for divination.

Vodou bottles

Vodou bottles are often decorated with fabric and sequins. Sometimes they are filled with rum, *kleren* (cane spirit), or wine, but chiefly they are left empty. These bottles are not repositories for the spirits, but rather offerings to honor the *lwa*. The bottles are often ornamented in the colors and symbols of an individual spirit, using cloth and sequins and sometimes incorporating the chromolithographs of the syncretic Catholic saints. Often, clear bottles are made with objects placed inside them, such as a doll's head and body. The bottles may be used as fetishes to ward off bad spirits, but can also be used by priests as tools of divination, divulging their secrets through the movements of the doll's eyes.

Vodou dolls

Dolls are placed on altars, but they are never malevolently pierced with pins, as in the common perception of Vodou. Black girl dolls in fancy dresses are often used to represent and honor Ezili Dantò. Some Vodou dolls are elaborate creations. Pierrot Barra, a Vodou priest and artist, created exquisite dolls as a way of paying homage to his beloved *lwa*. Discovered by ethnologists, these surreal and fantastic dolls have rapidly journeyed from the altar to the art gallery. Small handsewn cloth dolls, called messenger dolls, are used to transport covert messages to the spirit world, by binding to the doll a scrap of

paper on which the message is written. The dolls are then left at a crossroads or cemetery—which are considered to be gateways between the mortal and divine worlds—where they can transport the message to the spirit.

Paket kongo

Paket kongo are repositories for the spirits that are charged during a special ritual. They are cloth packets containing herbs and powders, bound with ribbons, and usually topped with feathers. *Paket kongo* are used for healing and protection and keep their powers for seven years. Each spirit has a different colored *paket kongo*, such as yellow for Loko Atisou, pink for Ezili Freda, and purple for the Gede family of spirits.

Some *paket kongo* are extravagantly decorated, perhaps topped with a doll's head, a bull's horns, or crossed forks.

Large black and gold paket kongo dedicated to Bosou, made by Jean Romy Jean Louis.

Sequinned bottle advertising Haitian roots band RAM.

Barbie doll in peek-a-boo coffin, created by Franz Barra.

A typical *paket kongo*, consisting of a cloth-bound base and a crown of feathers.

Sequinned bottle for Gede, with a skull on a purple background.

36

Doll sculpture by Franz Barra. Consisting of a bottle topped with a doll's head, it has a snake curving around its length in honor of Danbala.

Bottle containing a doll's head and feet used to ward off evil spirits.

Richly decorated blue *paket kongo*, entwined with a gold snake symbolic of Danbala, by Pierrot Barra.

Delicate silver *paket kongo*, encrusted with colorful stones and topped with blue feathers in honor of Ayida Wèdo, created by Pierrot Barra.

Vodou is one of the inspirational forces behind the rich abundance of painters, metalworkers, and flag-makers in Haiti. The role of priest and artist is often interchangeable, as the netherworld they inhabit, between spirit and material, is enlightened by dream and imagination. Art has become the material expression of the Vodou faith.

Vodou ArT

"Marie, Guardian of the Doves" by Alexandre Gregoire (below) is a traditional "naive" depiction of a seaborne saint surrounded by a host of black angels.

From temple to art gallery

Most Haitian art forms have their roots in Vodou practice—the paintings from temple murals, the metalworks from cemetery crosses, and the flags from the rituals. During the last fifty years, Haitian art has made the passage from the wall of the temple to the walls of the art gallery, and is now collected by dealers from all around the world. Haitian art is classified as "naive" or "primitive," due to lack of classical perspective and an unstudied, almost childlike style. De Witt Peters, an American schoolteacher working in Haiti in the early 1940s, can to a certain extent take the credit for having "discovered" Haitian art. While in Haiti, Peters noticed the unique and extraordinary art that surrounded him. He established the Centre d'Art in a beautiful old gingerbread building in Port-au-Prince, to create a

"Two Mambos" by Gerard is a strange and, possibly unintentionally, humorous depiction of two Vodou celebrants.

stable working environment for the untrained, often peasant, artists he attracted to the place. Peters discovered the doyen of Haitian art, Hector Hyppolite, an itinerant Vodou priest and painter. While driving through the town of St. Marc, Peters noticed a café door decorated with paintings of exotic birds. He located the artist, intrigued by both the style of the work and the prophetic sign above the door—"*Ici la Renaissance*" (Here the Renaissance). Hyppolite was invited to join other artists at the Centre d'Art, and was soon producing his singular and profound paintings on canvas rather than doors.

Abstract expressionism

The mid-1970s marked the emergence of abstract expressionism in Haitian painting, uninformed by art history. The artists, chiefly peasants, were still representing the *lwa*, but rather than showing them literally, in costume or as Catholic saints, the spirits were depicted as abstract energy, a spiritual force. The main group of expressionists were the Saint-Soleil Group, who lived in the mountains above Port-au-Prince.

"Twa Lwa" by St. Jacques Smith depicts three Vodou spirits in the abstract expressionistic style. The spirits have an amorphous and sexually ambiguous presence as ominous yet electric powers.

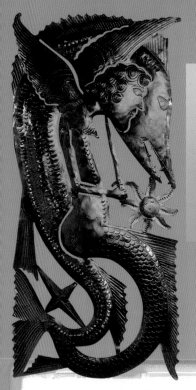

Lasiren by Jose Delpé depicts the divine mermaid riding the seas with the noble swordfish.

The blacksmiths of Vodou

The unique metalworks created in Haiti largely come from one small area in Croix des Bouquets, north of Port-au-Prince. The works are forged from recycled oil drums and shaped using chisels. Many of the metal sculptures are inspired by Vodou, some by Haitian folklore, and the more prosaic by the animal kingdom. Georges Liautaud, another protégé of De Witt Peters in the 1940s, was the founder and master of the metalwork movement. Liautaud, a blacksmith by trade, was discovered due to the strange crosses he had fashioned for the local cemetery. Peters persuaded him to try free-standing works, and once released from utilitarian boundaries, his imagination flourished.

Angel and Sword by John Sylvestre is a piece depicting an avenging angel, which is probably inspired by both Catholicism and Vodou.

Marasa by John Sylvestre is a representation of the sacred twins as two separate parts of a whole. Sylvestre produces his metalworks using characters from Haitian folklore and from Vodou.

Oungan by Julio Balan shows a Vodou priest with his sacred tools, the *ason* and the bell. Julio Balan is one of four brothers—the others are Romel, Jonas, and Joel—who all produce metalworks in a large atelier.

These dazzling sequinned tapestries are an art form unique to Haiti. The flags depict the pantheon of Vodou spirits, either symbolically using the spirits' *veve*, figuratively, or through the portrayal of the syncretic Catholic saint. The flags are thought to have military, Masonic, and religious origins, with roots in both Yoruba and indigenous Taino Indian beadwork.

Vodou

FlA9s of Haiti

Flag of Ezili Freda by Georges Valris, showing the spirit as the Virgin Mary.

Traditionally, the flags measure around 36 x 36 inches (90 x 90 cm), sometimes semi-sequinned on a colored background, though more predominantly covered solidly with sequins. They usually have a decorative border with the name of the spirit written in sequins, or beads at the top and the name of the artist written at the bottom. The artist's name is a more recent addition, which reflects the growing market in flags as *objets d'art*. An average flag will be covered with as many as 20,000 sequins, all applied by hand.

The flags, called *drapo sèvis*, play an important role in Vodou rituals, as they herald the beginning of the ceremony. Two flags hung on poles are carried by two *ounsi* called the *rèn drapo*, flag queens, from the *badji*, the sacred altar rooms, into the *peristil*, the main part of the temple where the ceremonies take place. The *rèn drapo* dance on either side of the *laplas*, the master of ceremonies, who carries a sword or a machete to honor Ogou Feray. The flag bearers bow to the four cardinal points and salute the priest or priestess, who kisses the flags and the hilt of the sword as a mark of respect. Traditionally, one of the flags used in the ceremony will represent Ogou Feray, and the other a second spirit that has special significance to the temple or society. The sparkle and glitter of the colorful flags serve to exalt the divinities and focus the congregation's meditation on the divine.

The spirit Agwe is always associated with boats and fishes. This traditional design is by Silva Joseph.

Flags as fine art

Although originally Vodou flags were made solely for religious purposes, their rich colors, lavish textures, and ancient symbols have now captured the attention of the art collectors' market. Both the Haitian expatriate community and art dealers have exported the exquisite tapestries to New Orleans, Miami, New York, London, and Paris. The secular flags produced for export are created without the decorative fringing that denotes a *drapo sèvis*, the sacred flags for use in ceremony. Their increasing currency in the art world has led to an explosion of creativity as artists have discovered the freedom to play with the form of the flags, though never deviating from the content.

Danbala is symbolically portrayed as the Catholic St. Patrick, with papal hat and snakes, by Jean Robert.

Bosou, the spirit of the sacrificial bull, is depicted by a *veve* on this flag by Georges Valris.

Yves Telemaque uses dramatic borders to emphasize the power of Rantretalacx, one of the Gede family of spirits.

This flag dedicated to Bawon Lakwa by Edgard Jean Louis is in the typical colors of Gede: black, purple, and white.

Papa Zaka, by Frere Noel, wears traditional peasant hat and clothes.

Edgard Jean Louis shows the spirit Gran Bwa surrounded by trees.

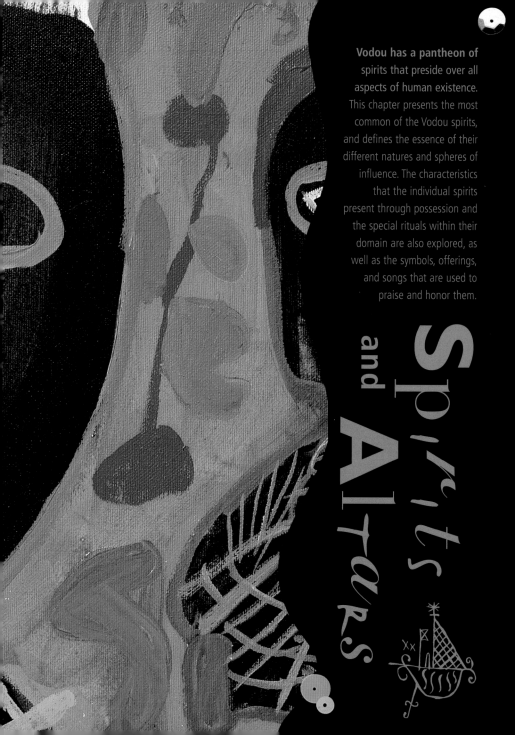

Vodou has a pantheon of spirits that preside over all aspects of human existence. This chapter presents the most common of the Vodou spirits, and defines the essence of their different natures and spheres of influence. The characteristics that the individual spirits present through possession and the special rituals within their domain are also explored, as well as the symbols, offerings, and songs that are used to praise and honor them.

Spirits and Altars

Vodou is a strange mixture of pantheism and monotheism. Adherents of Vodou acknowledge one superior god, known as Bon Dieu or Bondyé, who is beyond the reach of mere mortals and communicates through a pantheon of spirits, who act as divine messengers.

the Vodou pantheon

Vodou altar dedicated to Ezili Dantò in Bel Air, Port-au-Prince. Altars typically hold images of the spirit's Catholic counterpart and other symbolic objects.

The spirits, called *lwa* or *mistè*, are metaphysical forces that can enter the bodies of mortals through possession—during Vodou ceremonies, they are said to mount and ride the possessed person. When they arrive through possession, they sometimes give literal pronouncements and sometimes dispense a general collective healing. The spirits are thought to inhabit both the natural and the man-made world, including trees, streams, and stones, as well as dolls, crosses, and ritualistic objects. The spirits are the nexus between man and the universe, and reveal the invisible, the shadowland, and the deep mysteries of life.

Different spirits dominate various aspects of human activity, from sowing to harvesting, from love to war, and from birth to death. They relate the human condition from a Haitian perspective—the joys, pain, and toil of everyday life; the history and struggle of the slaves; and the cultural history of the African ancestors. All aspects of human experience are mirrored by the *lwa*. The spirits reflect kindness and malevolence, vengeance and protection, and famine and plenty. The pantheon is expanding all the time, and has regional and familial variations. Some of the spirits are the ancient gods from the animist religions of West and Central Africa, some were born of Haitian history, and some are simply blood ancestors. The form that the spirits take can also vary widely, from strongly anthropomorphized spirits with loud and colorful personalities to vague, abstract spirits who survey complex and mysterious domains.

Each spirit is honored by altars within the temple bearing objects, both sacred and profane, that are peculiar to that particular spirit. The spirits' altars are kept in small rooms, called *badji*, that are located around the perimeter of the temple. The objects placed on the altars range from chromolithographs of Catholic saints, and bottles of rum and perfume, to small boats, shovels, and dolls. Presents and offerings are left on the altars to reward the spirits for their help and guidance.

On the following pages you will find descriptions of the major Vodou *lwa*, detailing their distinctive characteristics and spheres of influence. Where notable, the form that each of the spirits takes during ceremonial possession is described, together with any specific customs and celebrations associated with that particular spirit. A summary chart appears on pages 50–51.

Characteristics of the Spirits

Name	Spheres of influence	Colors	Symbols
Papa Legba *(pages 52–53)*	Spirit of rituals, keeper of the gates, and guardian of the crossroads between the sacred and mortal worlds	Red, white	Cross, keys, walking stick, crutches
The Marasa *(pages 54–55)*	The sacred twins are associated with medicine, and act as protectors of children and fertility		Palm leaves
Loko Atisou & Ayizan *(pages 56–57)*	Patrons of the priesthood	White and red for Loko Atisou; white and silver for Ayizan	Red rooster for Loko Atisou; palm leaves for Ayizan
Danbala & Ayida Wèdo *(pages 58–61)*	Danbala, the supreme snake spirit, and his wife Ayida Wèdo, the mistress of the skies, are associated with wisdom and fertility	White for Danbala; white and blue for Ayida Wèdo	Snakes and eggs for Danbala; rainbow for Ayida Wèdo; white *paket kongo* for both
Ezili Freda *(pages 62–65)*	Spirit of love and beauty	Pink, pale blue	Checkered heart, white lamp with a white bulb, pink *paket kongo*
Agwe & Lasiren *(pages 66–69)*	King and queen of the ocean	White and blue for Agwe; blue-green for Lasiren	Boats, small metal fishes, paddles for Agwe; mirror, comb, trumpet, shells for Lasiren
Simbi *(pages 70–71)*	Patron of the rains and the currents of rivers, and master of all magicians	White, green	Snakes in a field of crosses, a well or spring
Papa Zaka *(pages 72–73)*	Patron of agriculture	Blue, red	A *makout*, pipe, machete, blue *paket kongo*
Ogou *(pages 74–77)*	Family of warrior spirits	Red	Machete, sword driven into the earth, red scarf and flags, red *paket kongo*
Ezili Dantò *(pages 78–81)*	Grand matriarchal figure	Blue, red, multicolored	Bowl of blood with knives, black dolls, blue *paket kongo*
Gran Bwa *(pages 82–83)*	Governor of the forests and part of a trinity of magicians who oversee initiation and healing	Brown, green	Strangely shaped lumps of wood or roots
Bosou *(pages 84–85)*	Associated with the fecundity of the soil	Red, black, white	Bull's head, horns
Gede *(pages 86–89)*	Family of spirits who act as guardians of the dead, and as mitigators between life and death	Purple, black, white	Skulls, black crosses, shovels, hot peppers infused with *kleren*

Offerings	Ceremonial possession	Favored trees	Catholic counterparts
Grilled chicken, sweet potatoes and plantains, bones, small bag containing *kleren*, tobacco and a pipe hung in a tree or doorway	Celebrants limp around the temple demanding a stick like a cantankerous old man	Calabash	St. Peter, St. Anthony, St. Lazarus
Baby goat stew wrapped in banana leaves, toys, candy, fizzy drinks, popcorn	The twin spirits pass on herbal remedies through possession		St. Cosmas and St. Damian
Rooster	These spirits preside over the entire ceremony and rarely appear through possession	Mapou for Loko Atisou; palm for Ayizan	St. Joseph for Loko Atisou
White chickens, white eggs, rice, milk	Celebrants fall to the floor, writhe and undulate like serpents, and dart their tongues in and out	Cotton	St. Patrick for Danbala; Our Lady of the Immaculate Conception for Ayida Wèdo
Sweet cakes, pink champagne, perfume, makeup, Virginia Slim cigarettes, white doves	Celebrants dance seductively, and flirt coquettishly and sometimes wantonly	Laurel	Mater Dolorosa de Monte Cavario
Champagne, liqueurs, cakes, white sheep, white hens for Agwe; white doves, perfume, mirrors, sweet white wine for Lasiren	Celebrants possessed by Agwe sit backward on a small chair and propel themselves around the temple using a small paddle		St. Ulrich for Agwe; Nuestra Senora de la Caridad and St. Martha for Lasiren
White animals	Celebrants are drawn to ponds and streams	Mango, calabash, elm	The Magi, Moses
Cassava bread, sugar cane, rice and beans, tobacco, *kleren*	Celebrants take a pipe and *makout*, roll up one trouser leg, limp around, and wolf down food in a corner	Avocado	St. Isador
Red rooster, rice and red beans, five-star Barbancourt rum, cigars, bulls	Celebrants wear a red scarf, brandish a sword, perform a fiery dance, curse like soldiers, and demand rum	Calabash	St. Jacques Majeur
Barbancourt rum, black pigs, fried pork, strong cigarettes	Celebrants become tense, clench their fists, and flash the eyes of a lion while uttering a hoarse "da da da"		Our Lady of Czestochowa, St. Barbara Africana, Our Lady of Mount Carmel
Leaves, flowers, tobacco, *kleren*, cornmeal, peanut cakes, cassava bread		Mapou	St. Sebastian
Fried beef	Celebrants snort and grunt and behave like a bull in a china shop		St. Vincent de Paul
Black rooster, black goat	Celebrants dress in purple and black, wear mirrored sunglasses, and strut and curse their way around the temple		St. Gerard

Papa Legba

Papa Legba is an ancient spirit who traveled with the slaves bound for Haiti on the ship from Dahomey in Africa. He is the spirit of rituals, the keeper of the gates, and the guardian of the crossroads.

ColoRs: Red, white

SymbOls: Cross, keys, walking stick, crutches

OffeRings: Grilled chicken, sweet potatoes and plantains, bones, small bag containing *kleren*, tobacco and a pipe hung in a tree or doorway

FAvored tree: Calabash

CathOlic Counterparts: St. Peter, St. Anthony, St. Lazarus

Papa Legba governs the threshold to the spirit world. As master of the crossroads, he can help you find the way if you are lost, and direct you to mislaid belongings. However, he also has a shadow equivalent, Kalfou, a trickster who walks with the spirits of the underworld, who can make you lose your way and bring disorder to your life. Papa Legba is the guardian of the entrances to temples and homes. He is the powerful spirit of communication between all spheres of life and death. The cross is his symbol, because it is at the apex of this cross that heaven and earth intersect. Papa Legba has several Catholic personas. He is related to St. Peter, who also holds keys; St. Anthony, the patron saint of lost objects; and St. Lazarus, because he walks with a crutch.

Ceremonial possession

Papa Legba is always the first spirit to be saluted during a ceremony because he holds the keys to Ginen, the homeland of the ancestors. The other spirits cannot visit earth until Papa Legba opens the gates. He is visualized as an old, infirm, lame man,

Papa Legba enjoys offerings of kleren, a type of cane spirit (above left); the keys to the crossroads are his symbol (right).

dependent on a crutch. During possession by Papa Legba, the celebrant limps around the temple demanding a stick like a cantankerous old man.

Customs and celebrations

A *makout*, a small straw bag, is often left in a calabash tree near the temple for Papa Legba, containing a bottle of *kleren*, some tobacco, and a pipe. He is also particularly fond of small piles of bones left at crossroads. There is a special dance to honor Papa Legba, which relates to the phallic stick dance performed for the African spirit Legba that is worshipped in Dahomey in Africa. A possessed man enters the temple with a twisted stick fitted to his crotch. The man twists one of his legs around the stick and performs a strange, grotesque dance before falling to the floor.

SOnG foR
Papa LeGba

Papa Legba, open the gate

for me so I can go through

When I return I will pay

honor to the lwa

Ceremonial sequinned flag depicting the veve for Papa Legba.

the MARASA

The Marasa are the sacred twins, the spirits of the first-ever children of Bondyé, and are protectors of children and fertility.

Spheres of influence:
Children, fertility, medicine

Symbol: Palm leaves

Offerings: Baby goat stew
wrapped in banana leaves, toys, candy, fizzy drinks, popcorn

Catholic Counterparts:
St. Cosmas and St. Damian

To revere the Marasa is to rejoice in the duality of the nature of man and the universe—the acknowledgment of the human and the divine, the mortal and the immortal, and the connection between the material world and the spirit domain. In Haitian society, twins are considered to have strong divine powers. However, even stronger powers are attributed to the next-born boy or girl within a family after the birth of twins. Such a child is called *dosou* if it is a boy, or *dosa* if it is a girl. The belief is that the sacred twins are just two of a trinity, and that the next-born child represents the restoration of the divine troika.

Customs and celebrations

Offerings for the Marasa are left in small pots that consist of two clay bowls melded together, like pottery Siamese twins. Part-sacred, part-secular, the Marasa form a bond between the earthly and the metaphysical realms, and are invoked early in a ceremony,

Siamese dolls used to represent the Marasa (left); a Vodou bottle bearing the images of St. Cosmas and St. Damian (right).

"Birth of the Marasa" by Jonas Balan. In Haitian society, twins are considered to have strong divine powers.

SOnG foR the MaRaSa

This is the food, this is the water

Take the family, if the family

falls on hard times

You take care of the family

You help the family

usually after Papa Legba. Through possession, the Marasa pass on the secrets of herbal remedies.

The month between December 6th (St. Nicholas's Day) and January 6th (the Epiphany) is the season of the twins, during which time a special feast called *mange Marasa* is held. The twins are often worshipped and fed on the feast day of the Massacre of the Holy Innocents on December 28th. This is to protect the living children, celebrate those that have died, and give solace to parents who have lost infants. Children are brought to take part in the *mange Marasa*, to stand in for the twins and consume the offerings.

Loko Atisou and Ayizan

Loko Atisou and Ayizan are the patrons of the Vodou priesthood. They are the ancestral spirits of the first-ever priest and priestess, and influential members of the Vodou pantheon.

Loko Atisou is the custodian of the temple, overlord of the priesthood, and guardian of the *ason*, the priest's sacred rattle and his most powerful tool. He is often symbolized by a fighting rooster and governs the *poto mitan*, the pole in the center of the temple that acts as a metaphysical highway for the spirits. He sanctions the divine passage between earth and heaven, enabling the spirits to journey from their spiritual domain to the temple. In a hymn to Loko performed during the ceremony, the words "the keys to the temple are in your hand" are sung.

Ayizan is the wife of Loko Atisou, and the protectress of the priestesses and female celebrants within a congregation. She is also the guardian of marketplaces, which are a common meeting point for Haitian women.

Colors: White and red for Loko Atisou; white and silver for Ayizan

Symbols: Red rooster for Loko Atisou; palm leaves for Ayizan

Offering: Rooster

Favored trees: Mapou for Loko Atisou; palm for Ayizan

Catholic Counterpart: St. Joseph for Loko Atisou

Ceremonial possession

As they represent the first-ever priest and priestess, Loko Atisou and Ayizan preside over the entire ceremony and

Loko Atisou is often depicted as a rooster.

56

rarely appear through possession. All celebrants have their own dominant spirit, called a *mèt tèt*, meaning master of the head, and it is Loko Atisou that reveals the identity of this dominant spirit through the officiating priest or priestess. During a ceremony, Loko Atisou and Ayizan are saluted soon after Papa Legba, but always preceding the remaining pantheon of spirits.

Customs and celebrations

Ayizan is invoked during ceremonies for spiritual birth and initiation. Her symbol is a palm frond, which is shredded during the ceremony and worn as a mask by the initiates. Loko Atisou, along with Gran Bwa, is a spirit of vegetation, and the sacred mapou tree is often hung with offerings for him.

When Vodou priests and priestesses are initiated, they are presented with seven paket kongo, including a yellow one for Loko Atisou.

Ounsi shredding palm fronds in honor of Ayizan during a ceremony in Bel Air, Port-au-Prince.

Danbala and Ayida Wèdo

Danbala, the supreme snake spirit, together with his wife Ayida Wèdo, the mistress of the skies, form the cosmic nexus between the sky and the sea.

These are ancient, primordial deities, holding a vestigial role within the Vodou pantheon dating back to creation itself. Often they are depicted with an egg, symbolizing their role in the dawn of life. They are associated with wisdom and fertility, and dwell within springs, pools, thunder, and lightning.

The origins of Danbala and Ayida Wèdo can be traced directly back to the religious animist practice in Dahomey, West Africa. Da was a snake god and divine force controlling life, and one of his avatars was Da Ayido Hwèdo. St. Patrick was elected as the Catholic counterpart for Danbala, as the saint is always depicted with snakes at his feet.

ColoRs: White for Danbala; white and blue for Ayida Wèdo

SymbOls: Snakes and eggs for Danbala; rainbow for Ayida; white *paket kongo* for both

OffeRings: White chickens, white eggs, rice, milk

FAvored tree: Cotton

CathOlic Counterparts: St. Patrick for Danbala; Our Lady of the Immaculate Conception for Ayida Wèdo

Wooden snake representing Danbala (above); offerings and sacred objects for Danbala and Ayida Wèdo (far right).

White eggs are used to represent the spirits' role in the creation of the universe.

The Creation Myth of Danbala and Ayida Wèdo

In the beginning there was a vast serpent, whose body formed seven thousand coils beneath the earth, protecting it from descent into the abysmal sea. Then the titanic snake began to move and heave its massive form from the earth to envelop the sky. It scattered stars in the firmament and wound its taut flesh down the mountains to create riverbeds. It shot thunderbolts to the earth to create the sacred thunderstones. From its deepest core it released the sacred waters to fill the earth with life. As the first rains fell, a rainbow encompassed the sky and Danbala took her, Ayida Wèdo, as his wife. The spiritual nectar that they created reproduces through all men and women as milk and semen.

The serpent and the rainbow taught humankind the link between blood and life, between menstruation and birth, and the ultimate Vodou sacrament of blood sacrifice.

Ceremonial possession

When celebrants are ridden by Danbala, they fall to the floor, writhing and undulating like serpents and darting their tongues in and out. Often during possession, celebrants will be impelled to climb up the *poto mitan* in the center of the temple, which is usually decorated with coiled snakes as a

Metalwork for Danbala and Ayida Wèdo by John Sylvestre.

homage to Danbala. The *ason*, the priest's most powerful tool, contains snake vertebrae, which provide the rattling noise that represents the voice of the divine serpent. It is often Danbala that appears to people in dreams, encouraging them to take up the *ason* and become priests.

Customs and celebrations

There is a yearly pilgrimage in Haiti to Saut d'Eau, a stunning waterfall that exudes a mist crisscrossed with minute rainbows. The pool into which the water pours is the domain of Danbala and other aquatic deities. The day of pilgrimage and celebration, July 16th, is shared with Ezili Freda, who appeared as the Virgin Mary nearby. The pilgrims pray and bathe in the holy waters of the cascades, often becoming possessed by Danbala. Small offerings and candles are left on the branches of the trees that surround the falls.

SOnG foR DaNɓaLa

The spirit works in the
water, it's Danbala
The spirit works in the
water, it's Danbala
Papa Danbala is the spring
Papa Danbala is the spring

"Danbala" by Fleurentus, depicts the spirit as a long, writhing snake with a man's head.

Ezili Freda

Ezili Freda is the goddess of love, and is concerned with all aspects of beauty. She adores flowers, jewelry, rich clothing, and fine perfumes. She is envisioned as a feminine, light-skinned mulattress, and is considered to be the epitome of charm. Ezili Freda is a little lazy, never working, and prefers to paint her nails all day.

ColoRs: Pink, pale blue

SymbOls: Checkered heart, white lamp with a white bulb, pink *paket kongo*

OffeRings: Sweet cakes, pink champagne, perfume, makeup, Virginia Slim cigarettes, white doves

FAvored tree: Laurel

CathOlic Counterpart: Mater Dolerosa de Monte Cavario

Ezili Freda loves jewelry, particularly with pink or blue stones (above); altar offerings and symbols for Ezili Freda (right).

Vodou priests place a chromolithograph of the Mater Dolerosa on Ezili Freda's shrine. This is a light-skinned Virgin Mary wearing a crown, and surrounded by jewels and finery. Ezili Freda is polygamous but wears three rings to signify her principal lovers. She is the mistress of Ogou, the concubine of Danbala, and the lover of Agwe.

Ceremonial possession

When Ezili Freda possesses celebrants they dance seductively, swaying their hips to and fro, and flirt coquettishly with the male members of the congregation. Sometimes she acts with wild abandon, covering the men with kisses

63

and rubbing herself against them. Ezili Freda is more reserved with the women congregants, merely extending her hooked finger toward them in acknowledgment.

As well as demonstrating love and benevolence, Ezili Freda can exhibit jealousy and vanity. She can be hopelessly demanding, always searching but never satisfied. Toward the end of a possession, Ezili Freda frequently collapses to the ground in tears, weeping for her unrequited loves and her unfulfilled dreams.

Many different types of images of the Virgin Mary are placed on altars to represent Ezili Freda.

Customs and celebrations

The Virgin Mary is said to have appeared on the top of a palm tree close to a small town in Haiti called Ville Bonheur, near Mirebalais. Pilgrims began leaving small offerings of food at the base of the tree for Ezili Freda. The local priest hastily ordered that the palm tree be cut down. A week later, the house of the priest burned down and soon after he died of a stroke. On July 16th, the Catholic holy day dedicated to the Virgin Mary, pilgrims from all over Haiti arrive at the waterfalls of Saut d'Eau near Ville Bonheur to bathe in the blessed waters there, which are also dedicated to Danbala and Ayida Wèdo. The pilgrims tie pink and blue girdles around trees close to the falls,

Blue sequinned bottle decorated with a red heart for Ezili Freda, the spirit of love.

SOnG foR Ezịlị Freda

Haughty Ezili, proud Ezili

Preening Ezili thinks she's something

Ezili is married, she's unlucky

Ezili is prostituted, she's unlucky

hoping that the luck and charm of Ezili Freda will shine on them.

Many men undertake a mystical marriage with Ezili Freda. Once married they must construct a bedroom for their goddess wife, decked in white, hung with lace, sprinkled with perfume, and housing the nuptial bed. The husbands must sleep alone in this room every Thursday night, when Ezili Freda will appear to them through their dreams. Her many consorts run the risk of invoking her wrath if they do not abstain from sexual intercourse, swearing, and drinking on Ezili Freda's special day.

Large pink and blue paket kongo for Ezili Freda, made by Jean Romy Jean Louis.

65

Agwe and Lasiren

Agwe and Lasiren are the king and queen of the ocean. They are called upon every time a boat is pushed out into the water. Agwe is visualized as a mulatto with green eyes, and is often referred to as Admiral Agwe. He is the custodian of ships, and is responsible for good catches and sea journeys. Agwe is allied to St. Ulrich, as the saint is usually depicted holding a fish.

The consort of Agwe, Mistress Lasiren, is a mermaid who possesses the wisdom of the water's depths. She is said to make an eerie music on the floor of the ocean, and is held to be the patron of musicians. Lasiren is a composite of feminine qualities from both Ezili Freda and Ezili Dantò. Like Freda she is a temptress, but like Dantò she is fierce and powerful. If offended, Lasiren will lure a person to a watery grave. She is characterized by dual aspects, like a fish of two colors. As Lasiren she is bewitching, white, and has long blonde hair, but her shadow countenance is Labalenn, the whale, who is black, shiny, and fearful, and represents the dark shadow that can be glimpsed deep beneath the waves.

Doll sculpture, in the form of a boat for Agwe, by Pierrot Barra (right); shells are symbolic of Lasiren (left).

COLORS: White and blue for Agwe; blue-green for Lasiren

SYMBOLS: Boats, small metal fishes, paddles for Agwe; mirror, comb, trumpet, shells for Lasiren

OFFERINGS: Champagne, liqueurs, cakes, white sheep, white hens for Agwe; white doves, perfume, mirrors, sweet white wine for Lasiren

CATHOLIC COUNTERPARTS: St. Ulrich for Agwe; Nuestra Senora de la Caridad and St. Martha for Lasiren

Ceremonial possession

When celebrants are possessed by Agwe, they sit backward on a small chair and propel themselves around the temple, puffing and blowing and using a small paddle. When the celebrants dance for Agwe, they undulate their bodies as if they were swimming under the water.

Many Vodou priestesses claim to have gained their skills from Lasiren. They dream that they have been taken down through the waters to the kingdom of the mermaid, where they received instruction in the priestly crafts, sacred rituals, and divine knowledge.

Customs and celebrations

Haiti is an island nation and therefore Agwe is an influential spirit, regularly fed and honored, especially in coastal temples. Ritual boats are hung from the roofs of temples in his honor. Agwe is invoked under a number of names, including "Shell of the Sea" and "Tadpole of the Pond." It is said that he can bestow all the riches, gold, and jewels that have been lost at the bottom of the ocean.

The mermaid spirit Lasiren beckons those at sea to return to Ginen, the tranquil ancestral home below the choppy waves of

SOnG foR Agwe

Alert the angels in the water

Beneath the mirror

Oh, he will see, he will see

Alert the angels down in the

water, oh he will see

Doll sculpture by Pierrot Barra, representing Lasiren as a mermaid.

SOnG foR Lasiren

The mermaid, the whale
My hat falls into the sea
I caress the mermaid
My hat falls into the sea
I lie down with the mermaid
My hat falls into the sea

Agwe is the custodian of ships, and is symbolized by boats on his altars.

life and the ocean. The ambiguity of her allure lies between the fear of drowning and a strong infantile desire to return to the Mammy Waters, the spiritual refuge. This is a choice that faced many of the slaves on the barbarous journey from Africa to the West Indies, as the sea was the only escape from the savagery of slavery. In order to overcome the fear of death, the sea soon came to represent a return to the homeland Africa and Ginen.

Services for Agwe and Lasiren take place on the coast, and the gifts and offerings are floated off on a small boat, which sinks and reaches their aquatic kingdom. The cloths that hold the food are blue and white, and the white sacrificial goat is dyed blue with indigo. There is a legend that if you are possessed by Lasiren during this ceremony, you dive to the seabed and return with seven fishes and seven coins.

"Agwe and Lasiren" by Jonas Balan, showing the spirits of the ocean with a catch of fish.

Simbi

Simbi is the patron of the rains, the currents of the rivers, and the master of all magicians. He abides in both the heavenly and the abysmal waters, the sweet and the salt.

CoLoRs: White, green

SymBOls: Snakes in a field of crosses, a well or spring

OffeRing: White animals

FAvored trees: Mango, calabash, elm

CathOlic Counterparts: The Magi, Moses

Simbi's spheres of influence inhabit the realms of both Danbala—the skies; and Agwe—the seas. In an urban environment Simbi oversees the flow of electromagnetic energy, from lights to telephones. Simbi's roots are believed to come from *zemi*, the indigenous Indian word for magic fetish. As the patron of magic, he oversees the assembly of *paket kongo*.

Ceremonial possession

Simbi is a withdrawn spirit, preferring the solitude of his watery abodes, and people possessed by him will be drawn to ponds and streams.

Chromolithograph of Moses, one of Simbi's Catholic counterparts (above); Simbi favors a number of trees, including the mango (above left), as he is fond of the mango fruit.

70

SOnG foR Simbi

Simbi in the two waters
Why don't people like me?
Because my magical
force is dangerous
They like my magical force in order
to walk in the middle of the night

Pale green paket
kongo for simbi.

Customs and celebrations

There is a yearly festival at Soukri in honor of the Kongo nation of spirits, where hundreds of celebrants submerge themselves in a local river in Simbi's honor. Ecstatic women lie among the reeds in the shallow waters while their white dresses flow in the strong currents. Fair-skinned children are warned against playing too close to springs for fear of being kidnapped by Simbi. The abducted children are taken under the water to work as servants. When the children are released from their aquatic prison and returned to the surface of the earth, they are rewarded with the magical gift of clairvoyance.

Ounsi honoring simbi while
bathing in the river at the
annual festival at Soukri.

Papa Zaka

Papa Zaka is the patron of
agriculture and wears the traditional dress of a peasant: a straw hat, denim suit, and red neckerchief. He always carries a small straw bag on his shoulder and wields a machete. He is a hard worker and has a large appetite, preferring the simple foods of the Haitian peasant.

ColoRs: Blue, red

SymbOls: A *makout*, pipe, machete, blue *paket kongo*

OffeRings: Cassava bread, sugar cane, rice and beans, tobacco, *kleren*

FAvored tree: Avocado

CathOlic CoUnterpart: St. Isador

Also referred to as Azaka, Mazaka, or Kouzen, the root of Papa Zaka's name is thought to be pre-Columbian, from the indigenous Taino Indian language, either deriving from *zada*, meaning corn, or *maza*, meaning maize. He functions as a reminder of a shared inheritance; of peasant roots, family links, and a deep relationship with the soil. Papa Zaka is responsible for ensuring successful crops and harvests, and is an especially strong spirit for his people, the long-suffering mountain farmers of Haiti. Papa Zaka is often depicted in paintings or on Vodou flags as the Catholic St. Isador, a devout farm laborer who was helped to complete

Blue sequinned bottle, in honor of Papa Zaka (right); Papa Zaka is the patron spirit of agriculture and usually wears a peasant's straw hat (above left).

his agrarian toil by guardian angels. François "Papa Doc" Duvalier, the dictator who ruled the republic of Haiti from 1957 to 1971, attempted to popularize his civilian militia within the rural community by dressing them as Papa Zaka. The country was thus tormented by legions of bullies, the Tonton Makouts, wearing denim suits and hats and red neckerchiefs.

Ceremonial possession

When celebrants are mounted by Papa Zaka, they take a pipe and *makout* (straw bag) and roll up one trouser leg to the knee. Papa Zaka is unsophisticated and inarticulate, but humble and kind, and limps around the temple and wolfs down his food in the corner. Papa Zaka articulates the urban caricature of simple peasants, often called Big Foot or hillbillies by the middle classes. When celebrants dance for Papa Zaka, they take on the lumbering gait of a peasant, or mimic hoeing and digging with their movements.

Expressionistic doll sculpture by Pierrot Barra, showing Papa Zaka smoking his traditional pipe; the machete is another of Papa Zaka's emblems, representing the spirit as a hard physical worker.

Ogou

Ogou is the family name for a congress of warrior spirits. Popular incarnations are Ogou Feray, Ogou Shango, Ogou Achade, and Ogou Balendjo.

ColoR: Red

SymbOls: Machete, sword driven into the earth, red scarf and flags, red *paket kongo*

OffeRings: Red rooster, rice and red beans, five-star Barbancourt rum, cigars, bulls

FAvored tree: Calabash

CathOlic Counterpart: St. Jacques Majeur

Ogou fights for justice but needs to be fed regularly or his hot, fierce temper can flare up in retaliation. He has dominion over fire and iron, the forge and war, and is the embodiment of masculinity. He is the protector of soldiers and the patron deity of barbers, road builders, truck drivers, and all who work with metal machinery.

Ogou is related to the Catholic St. Jacques Majeur, who is always depicted mounted on a horse and brandishing a sword. Ogou is visualized wearing a red military jacket decorated with gold buttons and epaulets, and is descended from Ogun, the Nigerian god of lightning.

Ogou worked alongside Jean-Jacques Dessalines and the Haitian slaves during their fight for independence at the beginning of the 19th century. In 1791 a Vodou ceremony was held in a dark forest called Bois Cayman, attended by hundreds of angry slaves. During a dramatic storm, the voice of Ogou spoke through the thunder and lightning, urging the slaves to battle. His sword split the

The sword is symbolic of the warrior spirit Ogou (above); altar offerings and symbolic objects for Ogou (far right).

75

SOnG foR Ogou

Fire spirit where are you going,

leave your children

When I remember Ogou Feray

I must be strong to call Ogou

He drinks but is never drunk

Ogou drinks but is never drunk

head of a black pig, and in its blood the priest wrote the words "liberty or death." This Vodou ceremony precipitated a 13-year struggle to eventual freedom from colonialist oppression.

Ceremonial possession

When celebrants are mounted by Ogou, they tie a red scarf around either their head or arm. They brandish a sword and perform a fiery dance that is both elegant and loaded with bravado. They shout and curse like soldiers, and demand rum. Their hands are washed with flaming rum, and sometimes they hold red-hot iron bars to prove that the possession is genuine. Ogou is welcomed by dousing the base of the *poto mitan* with flaming rum, liberally peppered with small piles of gunpowder.

Customs and celebrations

Every year a festival at Plaine du Nord, in northern Haiti, is held in honor of Ogou. In the center of this small town is a pond of mud known as Trou Sen Jak. Pilgrims arrive from all over Haiti on July 25th, the canonical feast of St. James. Most of the pilgrims wear blue outfits with red piping and red scarves, in imitation of Ogou's military status. They have come to say prayers, ask

Pilgrims bathing in the Trou Sen Jak mud pond in Plaine du Nord. This ritual bathing, in honor of Ogou, is held each year on July 25th.

Doll sculpture by Pierrot Barra depicting Ogou as St. Jacques Majeur, mounted on horseback and holding a sword.

Bottle of metal filings for Ogou, who has dominion over iron and is the patron spirit of metalworkers. The front of the bottle bears the image of St. Jacques brandishing a sword.

favors, and fulfill vows to Ogou. Stalls selling religious artifacts, food, and rum spring up all over the village, which soon comes to resemble a medieval fair. When pilgrims become possessed by Ogou, they roll around in the mud pond. It is said that the mud of the pond of St. Jacques has curative and magical powers.

Ezili Dantò

Ezili Dantò is the grand matriarchal figure within the Vodou pantheon. She is a hard-working mother, raising her child single-handedly. Fiercely independent with a stormy disposition, she would fight to the death to protect her offspring. Although she only has a single child herself, she is considered to be the spiritual mother of everyone.

ColoRs: Blue, red, multicolored

SymbOls: Bowl of blood with knives, black dolls, blue *paket kongo*

OffeRings: Barbancourt rum, black pigs, fried pork, strong cigarettes

CathOlic Counterparts: Our Lady of Czestochowa (the Mater Salvatoris), St. Barbara Africana, Our Lady of Mount Carmel

Ezili Dantò is visualized as a large, dark-skinned woman, attractive but not vain. Her essence is rooted in reproduction, and she is often invoked in affairs concerning either childbirth or conception.

Ezili Dantò's Catholic counterpart is the Madonna with child. The favored Madonna is Our Lady of Czestochowa, the black Madonna from Poland. This image was brought to Haiti by the Polish legions sent

Symbolic objects for Ezili Dantò in her favorite colors of red and blue, and bearing images of her Catholic counterpart, the Polish Madonna with the scarred face.

SOnG foR
Ezili Dantò

Ezili is the manbo
This temple is my house
This house is the house
of my spirit

to fight for Napoleon. The Polish ranks, sickened by the war against the slaves, mutinied and continued fighting on the side of the black slaves. The Polish Madonna is preferred due to her dark skin and the scars on her face, which are said to be wounds from the war of independence.

Ezili Dantò has a shadow incarnation as Ezili Red Eyes, who can be sharp and abusive toward her offspring. This is the fearless spirit that fought along with the ranks of slaves doing battle against Napoleon's army in their fight for

Ezili Dantò is the grand matriarch of the Vodou spirits. She is depicted as a large, dark-skinned woman, attractive but not vain. This statuette is adorned with multicolored beads in her honor.

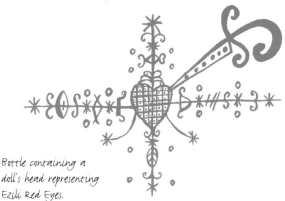

Bottle containing a doll's head representing Ezili Red Eyes.

freedom. Ezili Red Eyes inhabited the prostitutes who instructed the insurgent slaves to fight, and she drank *kleren* mixed with peppers and rum laced with gunpowder. Dantò's lover is Ogou, the noble and courageous warrior. However, just as Dantò has her downside, so too does her suitor, who at times can be an undependable, drunken, swaggering scoundrel.

Ceremonial possession

When Ezili Dantò enters the body of a celebrant, she is arrogant, harsh, and does not play games. The mounted person will be tense, fists clenched, and flashing the eyes of a lion. Ezili Dantò rarely speaks through possession, usually uttering a hoarse "da, da, da." It is said that she lost her voice at the end of the war for independence. The male slaves, with whom she had fought, did not trust her to keep their secrets, and cut out her tongue to silence her.

Customs and celebrations

Ezili Dantò frequently takes part in mystical marriages with the living, bestowing extra care and protection upon her spiritual partners. She weds women as well as men, and is therefore

considered to be the patron of lesbians. It is wise to marry Ezili Dantò if she demands it, as she can make her future consort sick until he or she consents.

Altar for Ezili Dantò in Bel Air, Port-au-Prince.

Ezili Dantò often demands a black pig, a traditional, indigenous animal that is difficult to find due to a U.S. eradication program in the early 1980s. Nowadays, Vodou priests must scour the countryside searching for a pig, perhaps hidden by peasants, to satisfy Ezili Dantò's voracious hunger.

GᴿᴬⁿBᴡᴬ

Gran Bwa is the governor of the forest and forms part of a trinity of magicians, along with Kalfou and Simityè. Gran Bwa symbolizes both the secrecy that dark forest cover can provide, and the secrets of herbalism that the forest can offer.

ColoRs: Brown, green

SymbOl: Strangely shaped lumps of wood or roots

OffeRings: Leaves, flowers, tobacco, *kleren*, cornmeal, peanut cakes, cassava bread

FAvored tree: Mapou

CathOlic Counterpart: St. Sebastian

Gran Bwa's spheres of influence are initiation and healing. He is represented as half-man, half-tree, with a stout, trunk-like body, branches for fingers, and roots for feet. He loves leaves and flowers for offerings. St. Sebastian has been chosen as his Catholic counterpart because of the saint's execution by arrows while bound to a tree. Ritual offerings for Gran Bwa are left in a *makout*, a straw bag, which is either hung in a tree close to the *peristil* in a country temple, or from the roof in an urban temple.

Customs and celebrations

An initiate must take a gourd and stay in the woods for a day with Gran Bwa in order to learn the knowledge of the leaf doctors. Adherents of Vodou regularly visit woods or forests to pay homage to Gran Bwa. The Haitian community in New York has now adopted Prospect Park in Brooklyn as the chosen sacred domain of Gran Bwa.

The trees in the yard of a temple are considered the sanctuaries of the gods, and are often painted and decorated. Small offerings and lit candles are placed in the recesses between the roots. The mapou, a silk cotton tree, is the most sacred of all

Gran Bwa is the governor of forests and is represented by pieces of wood.

SONG foR
GrAn BwA

Gran Bwa Zile Zile

Gran Bwa climbs to the wood

I am going to Gran Bwa

I am going to pick my leaves

the trees in Haiti. The tree was almost totally decimated during an anti-superstition campaign run by the Catholic Church in the early 1940s, which attempted to stamp out Vodou by destroying its sacred objects, drums, and temples, and even chopping down the beloved tree.

"Gran Bwa" by Gerard. Trees are the sacred repositories of the forest spirit.

Bosou

Bosou is a mighty bull spirit, represented with two horns. He is an unpredictable spirit, and, like his secular bestial counterpart, has a fiery and torrid temper.

CoLoRs: Red, black, white

SymbOls: Bull's head, horns

OffeRing: Fried beef

CathOlic Counterpart: St. Vincent de Paul

Bosou is associated with the fecundity of the soil. If Papa Zaka is the cultivator, then Bosou is the land on which he works. Bosou is the earth, the fruit, and the seed, and is associated with male virility.

The three-horned Bosou works with practitioners of malevolent magic—those who work with the left hand—and is invoked during the preparation of *baka*, small, malevolent monsters who wreak havoc and mischief.

Ceremonial possession

Although Bosou is represented by a bull, he is often considered to be a man, but a fierce-spirited man who prefers to eat beef. When celebrants are possessed by Bosou, they snort and grunt and literally behave like a bull in a china shop.

A painting of Bosou by Frantz Lamothe, depicting the spirit as a bull (above). Bosou is a powerful but fearsome spirit.

The three-horned Bosou is invoked by sorcerers during rituals that seek to wreak mischief and exact vengeance on others.

Sequinned flag depicting the two-horned Bosou, by Maxon.

Gede

The Gede family of spirits are the guardians of the dead and masters of the libido. They embrace the dual domains of human frailty and mortality, the creation and the conclusion of life.

ColoRs: Purple, black, white

SymbOls: Skulls, black crosses, shovels, hot peppers infused with *kleren*

OffeRings: Black rooster, black goat

CathOlic Counterpart: St. Gerard

This is not morbid, as it may be perceived in the West, but is in fact a celebration of the ancestral spirits and the continuation of tradition. Gede has strong powers of healing that are especially potent for children. The Gede family is presided over by Bawon Samedi, the lord of all Gede; Gran Brigitte, his red-eyed wife; and Bawon Lakwa, the Bawon's slow-witted brother and keeper of the graves. The family also includes Gede Fouye, who digs the graves; Gede Loraj, who protects those who died by the bullet; and Gede Janmensou, he who is never drunk. Gede wears the clothes of a missionary but has the appearance of an undertaker.

Miniature skulls and black candles are placed on altars in honor of the Gede spirits.

Ceremonial possession

When possessed by Gede, celebrants dress in purple and black, wear mirrored sunglasses, and sometimes brandish a large wooden phallus. They are lascivious and full of mischief, satirizing death and lampooning sexual intercourse. With their faces whitened like a corpse, they strut, thrust,

Coffins placed on Gede altars celebrate the presence of ancestral spirits at ceremonies.

87

Doll sculpture for Bawon Samedi, the lord of all Gede, by Jean Romy Jean Louis.

and curse their way through the congregation. The appearance of Gede is welcomed by the Vodou celebrants, as his behavior brings a vein of humor to the ceremonies.

Customs and celebrations

Gede presides over the cemeteries where his celebrations, called *fètdemò*, take place on November 1st and 2nd all over Haiti. On these two electric days, Gede escapes the confines of the divine spaces of the temples, and runs amok through the towns and countryside. People crowd into the graveyards to pour libations for Bawon Samedi at the foot of blackened crosses, which are decorated with skulls, marigolds, and candle wax. Such huge quantities of *kleren* are consumed that the air in the cemeteries is heavy with the liquor's aroma. The crowds chant lewd songs, and, in this atmosphere of wild abandon, many celebrants become possessed by Gede.

SOnG foR GeDe

Papa Gede is a handsome man

Papa Gede is a handsome man

He is dressed all in black

For he is going to the palace

Doll sculpture of Bawon Samedi by Pierrot Barra. The fabric and sequin-covered bottle is topped by a doll's head and fronted with a sequinned black cross.

Some people wear black and purple especially to invite possession.

Each year there is a special ceremony to feed the dead ancestors of the household, known as *mange mò*. The food must be strictly prepared by men only and contain no salt. The stew usually contains beef, pig's feet, maize, and scarlet beans. When the food is ready, it is laid out on a table in a room as if for a family. The room is then closed for several hours to allow the spirits to feast themselves in privacy. After a couple of hours, the head of the family knocks on the door and enters the room, collecting some of the food from the table into a large bowl. After saluting the four cardinal points with the food, it is then distributed among the children of the family. Another bowl of food is placed at the crossroads for Papa Legba, and some is hung in a tree for Gran Bwa. Once the dead have been cherished, the living can sit down at the table, enjoy the banquet, and continue to live in peace.

Most Vodou ceremonies are performed to feed and placate the spirits for the benefit of the whole community. However, the Vodou priest or priestess can also conduct rituals and charms that have a more direct benefit to individual celebrants. This chapter describes the complex preparations of many of these unique charms, and explores the application and benefits of the distinctive Vodou rituals that lie in the domains of initiation, marriage, harvest, and death.

Charms and Rituals

Magic **B**a**⊤**h**s** of Vodou

It is customary for adherents of Vodou to take magical baths, either in the temple, or in springs and rivers where spirits are known to live. To prepare a bath, you need to collect the ingredients associated with the spirit you are calling to work for you. These should then be mixed with water in a basin, and the potion rubbed over the whole body by a priest or priestess possessed by the relevant Vodou spirit. The bather is strengthened by the magical attributes of the plants, and the spirits are satiated by their sensual aroma. When bathing is finished, throw a coin into the basin, to pay the vessel and thank the water spirit.

ChArM Bath

For reconciling friendships, healing maladies, and procuring business

INGREDIENTS

1 gallon (4 liters) of water

Jasmine flowers

Orgeat syrup

Crushed almonds

Florida water

Holy water (from a Catholic church or religious store)

Champagne

Danbala and Ayida Wèdo preside over the charm bath. Danbala is thought to be the master of bath-givers because he plummeted into the abysmal waters—the kingdom of Ginen, the divine homeland of the ancestors—during the creation of the universe. The charm bath has wide-ranging powers, including the healing of deadly maladies, the reconciliation of broken friendships, and the procurement of new business and employment. In order to ensure the full potency of the bath, it should be taken on three consecutive days, beginning on a Thursday because this is Danbala's favorite day.

LaDy BaTh
For luck in love and money matters

The lady bath increases luck in love and improves your chances of winning money. It comes under the auspices of Ezili Freda, and her *veve* must be traced on the inside and outside of the basin in chalk. The bath should be taken once a year, and must be preceded and followed by the offering of a sweet dessert. Ezili Freda is particularly fond of rice cooked with milk and a sprinkling of cinnamon, or bananas fried with sugar. Use as much Florida water to scent the bath as you like, as perfume is an important element of Ezili Freda's toilette. Do not bathe for three days after having the bath in order to allow it to take full effect.

INGREDIENTS

1 gallon (4 liters) of water

3 bunches of basil

7 bell peppers (sweet peppers)

Pinch of *zo-devan* powder
(*Eugenia crenulata*)

Baume du commandeur

Tincture of benzoin

Florida water

Sweet dessert

Ib*o* B*a*т*h*

For luck and happiness

INGREDIENTS

1 gallon (4 liters) of water

2 pints (1 liter) of blazing alcohol

Pulped banana

Djon djon (dried mushrooms)

Crushed pineapple

7 holly leaves

Florida water

Holy water (from a Catholic church or religious store)

Spirits from the Ibo family, such as Ibo Lele or Ibo Sou Aman, must be summoned in order to concoct and execute this bath, which brings luck to the recipient. The Ibo spirits are from a small nation of spirits brought to Haiti from Africa by the Ibo people of southeastern Nigeria. The bath must be administered every day for seven days, always using the original solution. The power of the bath will diminish if any extra ingredients are added during the week-long operation.

Stress Bath

For relaxation and stress relief

INGREDIENTS

1 gallon (4 liters) of water

Handful of fresh or dried orange leaves

The stress bath is an herbal bath used for the relief of stress and tension, and as an aid to relaxation. It is a secular bath, and therefore is not presided over by any particular spirit. Boil the orange leaves in the water for half an hour, then let the liquid cool to room temperature. The recipient must sit with his or her head leaning back, while the solution is poured over the forehead and down the back. This is believed to draw bad blood and pressure away from the head. It is best to sit in a comfortable position and not to hurry the procedure.

Luck Bath

For well-being and good fortune

Ezili Freda presides over the luck bath. The ingredients should be placed in a bowl of fresh water—salt water must not be used, as it destroys the power of the luck bath—and the recipient's head bathed with the final infusion.

INGREDIENTS

1 gallon (4 liters) of fresh water
(do not use salt water)

Fresh basil

¼ pint (140 ml) of cow's milk

Cinnamon

Nutmeg

Pinch of tealeaves

Aniseed

Lèkos (powdered tree bark)

Florida water

INGREDIENTS

Salt or sea water

Kleren

7 vine leaves

7 bunches of fresh parsley

7 shallots

7 coins

Florida water

Bath to combat Misfortune

For help in times of trouble

Papa Legba presides over this bath, which should be prepared in a bathtub. First, the priest passes a crucifix, followed by a codfish tail, over the client's body, starting at the head. The priest demands that malevolent spirits leave the client's body, then plunges the client into the bathtub. The bath must take place on nine consecutive Fridays.

Magic
Lamps
of Vodou

Magic lamps are a popular method of procuring favors from the Vodou spirits. The lamps are constructed under the supervision of a priest or priestess using various receptacles filled with oil. The wick is suspended in the oil, either through a floating playing card or from crossed slivers of bone. Different substances are added to the oil, depending on the required outcome. Each lamp has a guardian spirit, and must be placed on an altar dedicated to that spirit, and prayed over and refilled with oil every day at the same time. The flame must not be allowed to die until the required result has been attained.

Charm Lamp

To attract a lover or business colleague

The charm lamp is used to attract and charm a potential lover, partner, or business colleague, and falls under the aegis of Ezili Freda, who reigns over territories of the heart. The main element of the lamp is the sheep's brain, which represents the will of the person whom you wish to attract. Place this in the shell and cover it with olive oil. The additional ingredients in the lamp possess either the attributes of sweetness or the properties of attraction. Thread the wick through the center of the Queen of Hearts card, and float the card on top of the oil. The lamp must be refreshed daily with olive oil and kept alight until the charm has worked.

INGREDIENTS

Coconut shell and wick

Queen of Hearts playing card

Piece of sheep's brain
(a piece of lamb will do)

Olive oil

Magnet

Cane syrup

Sugar

Honey

Florida water

Petals of jasmine and heliotrope

B**l**AcK **L**amp

To repel an enemy

The black lamp is exercised in order to repel an enemy, remove a disturbing neighbor, or assuage potent evil forces. Agwe is the guardian of the black lamp. Fill a crab shell or pumpkin gourd with the ingredients, then suspend the wick over them using crossed slivers of bone. The ingredients must be refilled every Friday for seven weeks and then thrown into the sea to satiate Agwe.

INGREDIENTS

Crab shell or pumpkin gourd and wick

Pair of bones

Castor oil

Pimen chen (a hot pepper, such as a bird's eye chili pepper)

Powdered lizard (or an item to represent the enemy)

Graveyard dirt or soil from a crossroads

Red precipitate (red oxide of mercury)

Soot or powdered charcoal

B**o**t**t**Le **L**amp

INGREDIENTS

Bottle and cork

Whiplash

Contents of the black lamp

To exorcise an enemy

The bottle lamp has the same ingredients as the black lamp, but they should be placed in a bottle rather than a shell or gourd. Suspend the wick in the bottle and light it. After it has burned for a whole day, blow it out and cork the bottle. Hang the bottle lamp in the yard and whip it every day with a whiplash. The bottle produces the same results as the black lamp, but the process is severely accelerated by the thrashing.

Work Lamp

To find employment and procure business

The purpose of the work lamp is to find employment or procure business. The lamp comes under the auspices of Papa Legba, and should be hung from the branches of his favorite tree, the calabash. If this is not possible, the lamp must be placed at the base of a small altar for Legba. Line a large calabash gourd with a piece of cloth pierced by seven small needles. Fill the gourd with olive oil and a dash of castor oil. Add some *baume du commandeur*, rose oil, and a small piece of beef heart. A sprinkle of gunpowder, a pinch of powdered madder, a drop of red wine, and a lump of lard complete the concoction. The last seven ingredients must be purchased at seven different stores.

Suspend the wick from a pair of thin bones balanced on the edges of the gourd, forming the shape of a cross. Prayers for Papa Legba must be recited each day at the same time, while gently stirring the oily contents of the lamp.

INGREDIENTS

Calabash gourd and wick

Pair of bones

Piece of cloth

7 small needles

Olive oil

Dash of castor oil

Baume du commandeur

Rose oil

Piece of beef heart
(a piece of beef will do)

Sprinkle of gunpowder
(a few match heads will suffice)

Pinch of powdered madder

Drop of red wine

Lump of lard

Eternal Lamp

To promote fertility and a healthy pregnancy

INGREDIENTS

Calabash gourd and wick

Queen of Spades playing card

Olive oil

Dash of castor oil

Small bunch of *zo-devan* leaves
(*Eugenia crenulata*)

Baume du commandeur

This lamp is assembled under the patronage of Ezili Dantò. It is believed to increase success in conception, and to bring health and protection during pregnancy. The oil should be mainly olive oil, with a little castor oil mixed in. Place a small bunch of *zo-devan*, Dantò's favorite leaf, in the gourd, then pour in the olive oil with a dash of castor oil. Blend in the *baume du commandeur*, which will bring an air of peace and tranquility to the dwelling where the lamp is to be kept. Thread the wick through the heart of the Queen of Spades playing card, float the card on the oil, and light it.

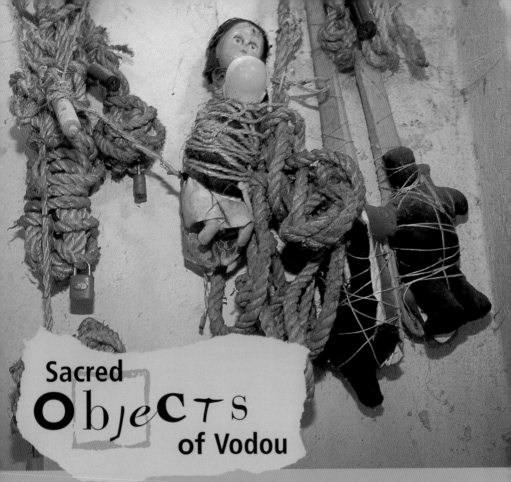

Sacred Objects of Vodou

Many objects are charged with divine powers from the Vodou spirits. Some of these objects are used in magical acts, some act as safeguards for the temple, and some are part of the ancestral process of birth, rebirth, and spiritual progression. If the objects come under the auspices of a particular spirit, they are usually kept in the temple's sacred altar room devoted to that specific spirit. Other objects may be carried, giving special protection to the person carrying them. Certain objects may have been inherited through the family line, and these are usually kept on a family altar within the home.

Oraisons

For good fortune and fulfillment of desires

Oraisons are Catholic prayers written on sheets of paper and sewn into clothes, bedding, or pillows in order to increase fortune and help fulfill desires. The prayers are sold in Haiti's Iron Market at Port-au-Prince. Prayers considered to have particular potency are devoted to St. Michael, patron saint of sea sickness sufferers; St. Bartholomew, patron saint of those with nervous conditions; St. Claire, patron saint of the poor; and St. Radegund, patron saint for those seeking protection.

Messenger Dolls

For petitioning the spirits

These are small handsewn cloth dolls that are used to transport covert messages to the spirit world. The clandestine missive is written on a piece of paper, and can either be pinned to the doll or bound around the doll with ribbon, string, or rope. If ribbon is used, it should be in a color associated with the spirit whose help is being sought. Leave the messenger doll at a crossroads or in a cemetery, as both of these locations are thresholds to the domain of the invisibles, and can be used to relay mortal despatches to the spirits.

PAKET KONGO

For protection and healing

Paket kongo are onion-shaped, cloth-bound packages containing a mixture of herbs and powders. They are made in various sizes and colors, depending on the spirit being represented. The packages are bound tightly with ribbons to protect and contain the spirit within, and are topped with feathers and sometimes adorned with mirrors or sequins. The *paket kongo* accord protection to the Vodou temple, and are used by the priest for healing by passing the package over the body of a sick person.

Paket kongo are made during a special ceremony that takes place under a full moon, and are bound under the aegis of Gede and Simbi. They contain the burnt and powdered flesh and feathers of a sacrificed rooster, mixed with the dried and crushed leaves of *twa-pawòl (Allophyllus occidentalis)*, *bwa-din (Eugenia fragrans)*, and *zo-devan (Eugenia crenulata)*. During preparation, the gourd containing the powdered mixture is placed on a *veve* for Simbi, the patron spirit of magic, drawn with ground coffee or ginger. The strings and ribbon that bind the magical packets must have been knotted seven times, and after seven years the powers of a *paket kongo* are spent.

Thunderstones

For magical powers

A thunderstone is a flat, oval-shaped stone revered for its magical powers. It is believed that thunderstones were formed during the creation of the universe, when Danbala cast thunderbolts to the ground, smashing the earth and the granite. Sometimes small pieces of mirror are glued onto the stone to increase its potency. The stone is often placed in a bowl of oil to prevent its power from draining away. Particularly strong stones are said to sweat, whistle, and even talk. In Haiti, thunderstones are nearly always inherited through family lines. They are rarely sold, as this would be perceived as a deep insult to the residing spirit, and an elaborate ceremony is essential if the stone is to be passed outside a family. It is certain that some thunderstones are actually pieces of stone spearhead used by the indigenous Taino Indians of Haiti. The Tainos deified the stones and passed them onto escaped African slaves when the two communities lived together in the hills of Haiti during the 16th century.

Paket kongo come in both male and female forms. The male form has a straight stem of feathers; the female form has looped arms below the feather crown.

Po тèт

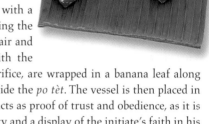

For storing an initiate's soul during life

Po tèt means, literally, a pot for the head. It acts as a vessel for an individual's soul, the *gwo bon anj*. A *po tèt* is usually a white china pot with a lid, which is placed next to an initiate during the initiation ceremony (see page 112). The hair and nail cuttings of the initiate, together with the burned and powdered remains of the sacrifice, are wrapped in a banana leaf along with some maize and candy and placed inside the *po tèt*. The vessel is then placed in the temple of the priest or priestess. This acts as proof of trust and obedience, as it is an acknowledgment of the priest's authority and a display of the initiate's faith in his integrity, since an unscrupulous priest could exercise power over a person through their *po tèt*. If initiates lose confidence in the priest, they may remove the *po tèt* from the temple.

The *po tèt* can also act as a focus for personal nurturing and ritual, perhaps to be bathed in cool water if its owner is feeling tense or irritable. After death, the *po tèt* is broken and the *gwo bon anj* released into the abysmal waters for a year and a day, before being reclaimed in the rites of the dead (see page 116). This period of oblivion is a prerequisite for immortality.

Govi

For holding the spirit of a deceased initiate

This is the vessel into which the *gwo bon anj* is placed a year and a day after death, during a ceremony called *wete mò nan ba dlo*, the extraction of the soul from the low waters (see page 117). The *govi* represents the cosmic womb of Ezili Dantò, where the *gwo bon anj* is to reside after returning from the abysmal sea. According to Vodou mythology, it is said that you are born animal, and are not truly human until you have been reborn through initiation. Once the *gwo bon anj* emerges from the abysmal waters into the *govi*, it has finally been transformed into a divine force. At the end of the ceremony, the *govi* are dressed in skirts of colored cloth. These represent the *mèt tèt*, the dominant spirit, of the deceased relative. Once the souls are satisfactorily ensconced in the *govi*, priests often find them heavier to carry back to the temple, where they are kept.

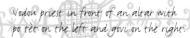

Vodou priest in front of an altar with po tèt on the left and govi on the right.

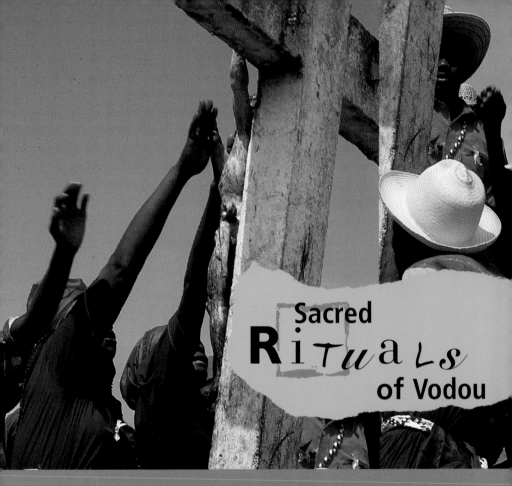

Sacred
R i t u a l s
of Vodou

In addition to the ceremonies for feeding the spirits, priests and priestesses must also perform rituals to deal with the community's more complex needs. These ceremonies serve the realms of initiation, death, spiritual marriage, and harvest. Initiation and mystical marriage strengthen the bonds between the congregants and the spirits they strive to serve, while the death rites warrant the passage of the mortal soul to divine immortality. Special ceremonies are also held to ensure healthy harvests, on both the land and at sea, to benefit the quality of life of the congregation.

Calendar  of Vodou events

January 6th	*Mange Marasa*	Day of the kings ceremony during which food offerings are given to the Marasa in special three-bowled pots and then distributed among mortal twins and children
February 25th	*Mange tèt dlo*	Ritual feeding of the springs
Good Friday	Souvenance festival	Major festival celebrating the Rada spirits held in Souvenance, near Gonaïves
July 16th	Saut d'Eau festival	Festival for Ezili Freda and Danbala, where celebrants bathe in a waterfall close to Mirebalais
July 25th	Plaine du Nord festival	Festival for Ogou, where celebrants bathe in a mud pool in a small town close to Cap Haïtien
August 14th	Soukri Kongo festival	Week-long ceremony for the nation of Kongo spirits, held at Soukri near Gonaïves
November 1st–2nd	*Fètdemò*	Festival of the dead for Gede, comprising two days of celebration held in cemeteries all over the country
November 25th	*Mange yanm*	Feast of the yams, a harvest ceremony held in rural Haiti
December 25th	Christmas baths and bonfires	People take baths and light bonfires to invigorate the spirits

The initiation ceremony is the intermediate spiritual state between congregant and priesthood. It precipitates the rise from the profane to the sacred, deepening the bond between the initiate and the spirits. During the ceremony, the novice becomes both servant and beneficiary of the spirits. It is a lengthy and elaborate process that tests the loyalty of the neophyte.

Initiation
ceremony

A divine marathon

The initiation ceremony, called *kanzo*, requires careful preparation. The novices take cleansing baths, eat mild foods, and abstain from alcohol and coffee for three days preceding the divine marathon. Ayizan, the spirit of the original priestess, is honored in a ceremony called *chire Ayizan*, during which palm leaves are ripped into thin strips hanging from the central stalk. These are used to whip the legs of the initiates gently while they receive instructions of their duties. This ritual precedes a seven-day period of confinement in a room called a *djèvo*, the spiritual womb from which the initiate will be reborn.

Loko Atisou, the spirit of the original priest, will have already revealed the identity of the *mèt tèt*—the novice's dominant *lwa*—to the priest, and the *djèvo* will be decorated with sacred symbols, objects, and food offerings to gratify that particular *lwa*. Inside the *djèvo*, the novices lie on their left side on a bed of leaves, with a large stone for a pillow. The novices endure this state, neither speaking nor moving, and only calling for assistance with a bell, for a week. A *po tèt* (see page 108) is laid next to the harsh

small clay pots on metal stands are used for the boule zin ceremony.

An ounsi tending the firing of the boule zin, the ceremony of the burning pots, during an initiation ritual.

bed. Nail trimmings and a lock of the initiate's hair are placed inside the *po tèt* to create the *gwo bon anj*, the novice's soul. A compress of wine-soaked bread, maize, milk, and cooked rice, sprinkled with chicken's blood and syrup, is wrapped in leaves and tied to the initiate's head. This helps to establish the *mèt tèt* in the head of the novice. The neophyte must survive the week on a diet of unsalted dried tripe and chicken, washed down with corn soup and water.

Boule zin

The *boule zin* ceremony is performed the evening before the initiate's release from confinement. This is literally a baptism of fire that precedes the divine rebirth. Small clay pots are placed on metal stands beneath which stick fires are lit. The pots are used to cook hot maize dumplings, which are then pressed onto the palms and soles of the novices, who are brought out into the temple covered with white sheets. Once the novices have retreated back into the sanctuary, the pots are fired up with more oil, the stick fires replenished, and they are set spectacularly ablaze. This sets the congregation alight with energy and possession.

The next day the initiates leave their sanctuary, clean, wearing new robes of pure white and straw hats, and holding shredded palm leaves over their faces as masks. They are baptized with water sprinkled from a leafy branch, and the celebratory dancing and drumming continue all night long.

mystical
Marriage

An initiate may undertake a mystical marriage
with a spirit in order to deepen and strengthen the
relationship. Principally, but not invariably, union takes place
between the celebrant and his or her dominant spirit. Sometimes
another spirit can demand betrothal, through the dreams of the future
bride or groom. The spirits most likely to undertake matrimony with
mortals are Ezili Freda, Ezili Dantò, Danbala, Ogou, and Agwe.

The marriage ceremony

Vows are taken and rings are exchanged, as in an earthly
marriage, and the mortal partner promises to put one
night per week aside as a devotion to the divine consort.
On this night, the initiates must sleep alone, often in a
specially prepared single bed, and wait for their spiritual
reverie with their sacred husband or wife. If they take
part in sexual intercourse with a mortal on this night,
they risk inflaming the fury of their spirit partner.

The marriage ceremony can be expensive, as the
celebrant must provide the wedding trousseau and
rings, and the cakes and drinks for the reception.
On the prescribed day, an altar is set up in
the courtyard of the temple, and laden with
cakes, candles, and holy water. The officiating priest is called the *prèt
savann*, or bush priest, and begins the ceremony by baptizing the
wedding gown and drawing the *veve* of the participating spirit on
the floor of the temple. The spirit arrives at the ceremony
through possession. Sometimes the mortal bride or groom is ridden by the divine spouse, or sometimes a third party acts as a proxy
with the betrothed and receives the honored spirit. Two godparents

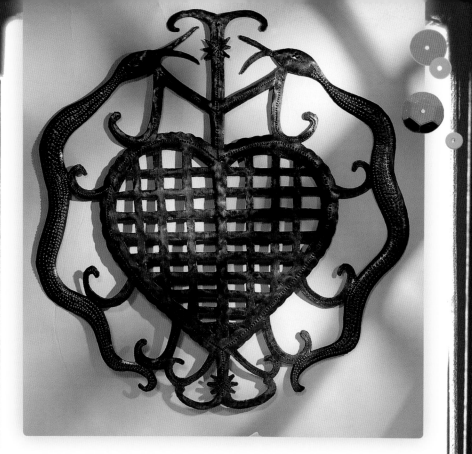

flank the mortal bride or groom and act as witnesses to the sacred wedlock.

The *prèt savann* asks the spirit if he or she will take the mortal as husband or wife and promise to protect them. The priest then asks the mortal if they take the spirit as their husband or wife, promising to be faithful for one night per week. The godfather places two rings on the finger of the mortal spouse as the priest reads out the divine marriage sacraments. The witnesses sign the certificate and the mortal spouse

During the ceremony, offerings are placed on altars bearing symbols of the relevant spirit, such as a snake for Danbala.

eats the special foods of his or her spiritual husband or wife. For example, this can be white eggs and flour for Danbala, or sweet cakes and syrup for Ezili Freda. The conjugal celebrations continue with singing and dancing, and the wedding cake is then shared among the congregation.

When an initiate dies, his or her family must call the priest or priestess to the house immediately in order to begin the elaborate death rituals. The deceased's soul and guardian spirit are released from his or her body. The soul must sink into the abysmal waters, the kingdom of Ginen, and reside there for a year and a day. During this divine purgatory, the person's soul will gain immortality, deification, and sacred knowledge in order that it return to earth and benefit its descendants with newfound wisdom and power.

DeAth
rites

The *ti bon anj*, the life force, takes flight on the final breath of the mortal to rejoin the cosmos. The ritual that releases the soul, the *gwo bon anj*, and the guardian spirit, the *mèt tèt*, is called the *desounen*, meaning forcing out of the soul. The priest spits a spray of *kleren* (cane spirit) over the body, anointing the four cardinal points, and lights a candle for the deceased. While shaking his *ason*, the sacred rattle, he implores the *mèt tèt* and the *gwo bon anj* to abandon the corpse. At the point of departure, the priest becomes possessed by the *mèt tèt*, and breaks the *po tèt*, the pot into which the soul is placed during initiation, to sanction the soul's descent into Ginen.

The priest sprays kleren (above) over the deceased's body and lights a candle (right) to persuade the soul to depart.

Protecting the body

The priest also prepares the coffin by placing the branches of a sesame plant with the body. This is to prevent a sorcerer from digging up the coffin, as he is obliged to count any seeds in a coffin before commencing his dark work, but the sesame plant holds so many seeds that the sorcerer cannot count them before daybreak. The priest stuffs the nose to prevent breathing, and binds the legs to prevent the cadaver from ever walking the earth again. The corpse is then bathed in a liquor of water, alcohol, and infusions of orange, mint, and sour sap leaves.

Reclaiming the soul

After a year and a day, the *gwo bon anj* must be reclaimed in a ceremony called *wete mò nan ba dlo*, removing the dead from the low waters. A large bath of water, symbolizing the abysmal waters, is placed in the courtyard of the temple. A tent is built around the bath and covered with a white sheet. Once the drums begin, white-clad *ounsi* enter the *peristil* carrying empty *govi*, clay pots for accommodating the souls (see page 109), on their heads. They lie on mats made of dried banana leaves with their heads inclined toward the covered bath. A number of souls are reclaimed during each ceremony, as many families pool their resources in order to reduce the expense.

Inside the tent, the priest beseeches the souls to withdraw from the abysmal waters. He recites the names of the dead, and rattles his *ason* over the surface of the water. One by one, the *ounsi* are wrought with convulsions as the *govi* are charged with the *espri*, the restored souls. This can be a lengthy, draining, and tortuous process, as not all *espri* return with celebration and happiness—some can return in anger and pain. Once all the *govi* have been filled, the relatives take them home to be placed on family altars.

A year and a day after the release of the soul from the deceased, the priest uses his ason (above) to draw the soul back from the abysmal waters into a govi (left), a clay pot that is kept on the family altar.

117

feast of the Yams

The feast of the yams is held every year preceding the harvest. It is primarily a rural celebration, and large extended families gather together for the rituals and feasting. The yam is held in high regard as a staple food in Haiti, as it was brought over from the homeland Africa. The feast of the yams both acknowledges the bond with the African ancestors and thanks the spirits for the fecundity of the soil.

Putting the yams to bed

The ceremony, called *mange yanm*, meaning eating the yams, usually takes place over a period of two days. The first day is known as *kouche yanm*, the putting to bed of the yams, and bestows the vegetables with mystical powers. The yams are placed on the *poto mitan* and surrounded by bananas and dried fish. The food is sprinkled with libations of rum and carried into the altar room by a procession of *ounsi*. They are laid down on a *veve* drawn in cornmeal and covered with mombin leaves and a shredded palm leaf.

The rising of the yams

The ceremony that takes place the next day is called *leve yanm*, the rising of the yams. Having spent the night in the realm of the spirits, the yams are now sacred. Chickens and goats are sacrificed and laid next to the yams in the altar room. Crosses are drawn on the food using cornmeal mixed with ash, and libations are poured. The dead of Haiti and Africa are invoked, together with ancestral and familial spirits. Each member of the family takes a turn cleaving the yams apart with a machete to prepare them for cooking. After much singing and dancing to praise the spirits, the yams are boiled along with the dried fish. Once a portion of the stew has been buried for the spirits, the rest is shared among the congregation. Now the peasants are free to harvest their yam crop without fear of insulting their capricious gods.

The bark of Agwe is a wooden raft, usually painted blue and ornamented with nautical motifs. It is laden with white rice, melons, iced cakes, flowers, whiskey, champagne, and rum. Agwe is particularly fond of foreign liquors through his many ocean voyages. The raft is floated out into the sea and sunk so that Agwe can feast on the banquet at the bottom of the ocean.

the Bark of Agwe

Preparing the raft

The raft is prepared in the temple on the night preceding the ceremony and guarded by *ounsi*. The ceremonial drums are painted blue and white for the event. The skins are made more taut than usual so that they may resonate to the floor of the sea, summoning Agwe and his consort Lasiren. On the day of the ceremony, the raft is transported to the coast, usually on the back of a truck also containing the drums, flags, *ason*, cornmeal, candles, sacrificial animals, and the whole congregation. The raft is laid down beside the ocean and *veve* are drawn around it in cornmeal. A conch shell is blown to signify the start of the ceremony. The raft is then loaded onto a sailboat to transport the congregation, the drummers, the *ounsi*, and the priest to Zile, the sacred spot where they will release the seaborne offering for the marine spirits.

Awakening Agwe

As the journey commences, the priest lights a small oil lamp in a white cup and the drummers begin their rhythmic awakening of Agwe. Once the boat reaches Zile, a small reef off the coast of Haiti, a snow-white lamb, two white chickens, and two white doves are cast into the sea, followed by the food-laden raft. The drumming and singing continue until the sailboats return to the shores, where the ceremony continues. The priest must keep a sharp eye on his congregation during the return journey, as possessed celebrants have been known to dive into the sea.

Divination

All Vodou priests and priestesses perform divination as part of their sacred duties. This usually involves the use of special objects, most commonly shells, leaves, and cards.

The most traditional method of divination employs seven small shells, which are charged with special powers during a ceremony that includes the sacrifice of a rooster. The shells are kept in a small wallet, which must also contain the tiny skull and tibias of the sacrificed bird. When questioning fate, the priest or priestess must invoke the spirit Simbi, the patron of magic, while shaking the shells in his or her hands. The shells are then thrown onto a flat corn sieve containing a candle, a magic stone, and a sacred bead necklace. The pattern that the shells make on the sieve form the basis for the prediction.

Priests also use playing cards for disclosing the future. The cards are dealt onto a corn sieve containing a lit candle and sacred stones that have been passed through the flames of burning *kleren* (cane spirit) before commencing the reading. The flame of the candle enables the priest to communicate with the spirits and fathom the true significance of each card. Priests can also use tealeaves, coffee residue, or cinders as a window on the future. As well as indicating the future prospects of the sitter, the priest will use divination to indicate the attitudes and needs of the spirits. If sitters have been neglecting their duties to the *lwa*, they will be advised to make food offerings, a sacrifice, or, in severe circumstances, hold a ceremony.

finding 18th-century
TʀeɑSuʀe

As the political situation in Haiti became increasingly unstable for the the plantation owners during the time of the slave uprisings, it is believed that many of them buried their riches due to fear of looting. The spirits are often consulted to discover the whereabouts of this treasure.

The slave who was chosen to dig the hole for the casket of gold would also be digging his own grave. Through fear of discovery, the plantation owner would kill the slave and bury his body with the fortune. It is believed that the spirit of the slave remains with the booty, and he can lead his descendants to the treasure. Usually the slave's spirit contacts a relative through dreams, or by prophesy through possession, to reveal the spot where the treasure can be found. Care must be taken while digging for the treasure as the protecting spirit is often angry, wrathful, and extremely dangerous. It is therefore important to have a priest in attendance to distract and placate the guardian spirit.

Glossary

ASON Sacred rattle used to call the spirits

BADJI Altar room in the temple

BAKA Little demon

BA TAMBOU MANGE Feeding the drums ceremony

BAT TAMBOU Name often used to refer to Vodou ceremonies, meaning beating the drums

BAUME DU COMMANDEUR Balm used as an ingredient in Vodou charms, widely available from magical botanicas in Haiti

BIZANGO Secret society

BÒKÒ Sorcerer

BOULA Smallest drum of the Rada nation

BOULE ZIN Ceremony of the burning pot

BWA-DIN One of the plant ingredients of Vodou charms; Latin name *Eugenia fragrans*

CHANTE LWA Ceremonial singing

CHIRE AYIZAN Ceremony in honor of Ayizan during which palm leaves are shredded for the initiation ceremony (*kanzo*)

CHROMOLITHOGRAPH Colored paper picture of a Catholic saint

DESOUNEN Ritual for releasing both the soul (*gwo bon anj*) and the guardian spirit (*mèt tèt*) from a body after death

DJÈVO Confinement room for initiation ceremony

DJON DJON Dried mushrooms

DOSOU/DOSA Male/female offspring after the birth of twins

DRAPO Flag

DRAPO SÈVIS Vodou flag used in ceremonies

ESPRI Soul restored from the abysmal waters

FÈTDEMÒ Feast of the dead, the celebrations held for Gede

GINEN Homeland of the spirits, generic term for Africa

GOVI Clay pots used to store souls after their return from the abysmal waters

GWO BON ANJ Soul of the initiated

KANZO Initiation ceremony

KLEREN White cane spirit

KONFYANS Assistant to the priest or priestess

KOUCHE TAMBOU Part of a ritual to reinvigorate the energy of the sacred drums, meaning putting the drums to bed

KOUCHE YANM Putting the yams to bed ceremony, the second part of the feast of the yams

KREYÒL French *patois* spoken in Haiti (Creole)

LANGAJ Ancient African language, long forgotten but words of which are incorporated into Vodou songs

LAPLAS Master of the sword who leads the flag parade during ceremonies

LÈKOS Powdered tree bark

LEVE YANM Rising of the yams ceremony, the third and final part of the feast of the yams

LWA Spirit

MACHÈ FEY Leaf market in Haiti where many of the plant ingredients used in Vodou charms and rituals can be bought

MAKANDEL Secret society

MAKOUT Straw bag

MANBO Priestess

MANMAN Largest drum of the Rada rites, literally means "mother"

MANGE LWA Feeding the spirits—for example, the feast known as *Mange Marasa* held in honor of the Marasa spirits

MANGE MÒ Ceremony to feed the dead ancestors of the household

MANGE TÈT DLO Ritual feeding of the springs

MANGE YANM Feast of the yams

MAPOU Sacred silk cotton tree

MÈT TÈT Guardian spirit

MISTÈ Spirit

OGAN Metal plate or bell that is hit with an iron rod used to keep the beat for the drummers

ORAISONS Catholic prayers written on sheets of paper that are used to petition the spirits' help

OUNFÒ Vodou temple, including both altars and ceremonial space

OUNGAN Priest

OUNJENIKON Leader of the chorus

OUNSI Singer and dancer initiate within the congregation

PAKET KONGO Cloth-bound package containing spiritual powers

PERISTIL Ceremonial space within a temple

PETWO Family of "hot," turbulent spirits

PIMEN CHEN Small hot red peppers

PO TÈT China repository for an individual's *gwo bon anj*

POTO MITAN Central pole of the *peristil*

PRÈT SAVANN Bush priest, who often conducts mystical marriages

RADA Family of "cool," gentle spirits

RÈN DRAPO Flag queens who carry the sequinned Vodou flags during ceremonies

SEGON Second, middle-sized drum of the Rada rites

SÈVIS Ceremony

SIMITYÈ Cemetery

TI BON ANJ Life force

TWA-PAWÒL One of the plant ingredients of Vodou charms; Latin name *Allophyllus occidentalis*

VEVE Ritual drawing that depicts a spirit

VLENBLENDENG Secret society

VOYE LAMÒ Most feared act of a sorcerer, meaning to send death

WANGA Object, package, or poison created by sorcerer to cause harm to others

WETE MÒ NAN BA DLO Extraction of a dead initiate's soul from the abysmal waters to be contained in a *govi* and placed on an altar

ZOBOB Secret society

ZO-DEVAN One of the plant ingredients of Vodou charms; Latin name *Eugenia crenulata*

ZOMBI An individual who is poisoned, appears to be dead, and later is "resurrected" by a sorcerer, who then controls the *zombi*'s will and actions

NOTE ABOUT VODOU INGREDIENTS
Although the ingredients used in the charms and rituals in this book are widely available in Haiti, they are more difficult to find outside the country. Some cities outside Haiti do have specialty Vodou stores, which stock a wide variety of the ingredients used by Vodouists. Other sources of ingredients may be found by searching for Vodou botanicas on the internet.

Index

Page numbers in *italics* refer to illustrations

Credits

AUTHOR'S ACKNOWLEDGMENTS

This book is dedicated to Ranu Mukherjee with thanks for her friendship, companionship in Haiti, and assistance in the research for this book. Thanks also to Charles Arthur, Maggie Roberts, Rich Honour, John Cussans, Linette Frewins, Laurie Richardson, Ian Murray, Richard Morse, Markel Thylefors, Cinders Forshaw, and Edgard Jean Louis.

PICTURE CREDITS

Quarto would like to acknowledge and thank the following for supplying pictures reproduced in this book:

KEY: *l* left, *r* right, *c* center, *t* top, *b* bottom

p7 Leah Gordon, p11 J-L Charmet, p12 J-L Charmet, p19 Leah Gordon, p20*t&b* Leah Gordon, p21 J-L Charmet, p25 Leah Gordon, p26 Leah Gordon, p29*b* Leah Gordon, p30 J-L Charmet, p31 Leah Gordon, p48 Leah Gordon, p57*r* Leah Gordon, p71*b* Leah Gordon, p76 Leah Gordon, p81 Leah Gordon, p92 Leah Gordon, p98 Leah Gordon, p104 Leah Gordon, p108*b* Leah Gordon, p110 Leah Gordon, p113 Leah Gordon

All other photographs and illustrations are the copyright of Quarto. While every effort has been made to credit contributors, Quarto would like to apologize should there have been any omissions or errors.

SPECIAL THANKS

Quarto would also like to express thanks to the following people for kindly allowing us to photograph items from their collections for reproduction in this book:

Charles Arthur pages 15 (large boat), 36*tr*, 69*tr* (large boat)

John Cussans page 53

Annabel Edwards & Leah Gordon pages 1, 40*tl,bl&br*, 41, 43, 44 (all), 45 (all), 55, 69*bl*

Linette Frewins pages 14, 54*br*, 64*l*, 67, 78 (smaller bottle)

Leah Gordon pages 2, 4, 8–9, 13*t&br*, 15 (small boat), 22*tl&bl*, 23*tl&bl*, 24*t&b*, 27, 28*c*, 29*tl&tr*, 34, 36*tl,bl&br*, 37*tr&br*, 38, 39*t&b*, 46–47, 49, 56, 57*bl*, 58, 59 (*paket kongo*), 61, 63, 64*tr*, 66, 69*tr* (small boat), 71*tr*, 72*l&r*, 73 (doll sculpture), 75 (doll, bottles, and flag), 77*bl&tr*, 78 (except smaller bottle), 79, 83*bl*, 84*l&r*, 85, 86 (all), 87, 90–91, 94*l*, 105, 106–107 (*paket kongo*), 116*tl*, 120

Rich Honour page 17

Ranu Mukherjee pages 13*bl*, 35, 37*tl*, 59 (doll sculpture), 65, 75 (*govi*), 80*l*, 89, 109*tr*, 112, 116*bl*

Paul Ricard page 73 (machete)

Maggie Roberts pages 37*bl*, 54*bl*, 68, 88

Maggie Roberts & Rich Honour pages 60*b*, 115

BIBLIOGRAPHY

Divine Horsemen: The Living Gods of Haiti; Maya Deren; Documentext; 1953 & 1970

The Drum & the Hoe: Life & Lore of the Haitian People; Harold Courlander; University of California Press; 1960

The Faces of the Gods: Vodou & Roman Catholicism in Haiti; Leslie G. Desmangles; Chapel Hill, University of North Carolina Press; 1992

Flash of the Spirit: African & Afro-American Art & Philosophy; Robert Farris Thompson; Vintage, 1984

Forgerons du Vodou: Voodoo Blacksmiths; Alan Foubert; Cidihca.Deschamps.Ulys; 1990

Haitian Vodou Flags; Patrick Arthur Polk; University Press of Mississippi; 1997

Haiti, History and the Gods; Joan Dayan; University of California Press; 1995

Infectious Rhythm; Barbara Browning; Routledge; 1998

Libète: A Haitian Anthology; Charles Arthur (editor); Latin American Bureau; 1999

Mama Lola: A Vodou Priestess in Brooklyn; Karen McCarthy Brown; University of California Press; 1991

Sacred Arts of Haitian Vodou; Donald Cosentino (editor); UCLA Fowler Museum; 1995

Secrets of Voodoo; Milo Rigaud; City Lights; 1985

Sequin Artists of Haiti; Tina Girouard; Contemporary Arts Center of New Orleans; 1994

The Serpent & the Rainbow; Wade Davis; Collins; 1986

Spirits of the Night: The Vaudun Gods of Haiti; Selden Rodman; Spring Publications Inc; 1992

Tracing the Spirit: Ethnographic Essays on Haitian Art; Karen McCarthy Brown; Davenport Museum of Art; 1995

Vodou Things: The Art of Pierrot Barra & Marie Cassaise; Donald J. Cosentino; University Press of Mississippi; 1997

Voodoo in Haiti; Alfred Métraux; Schocken Books; 1959 & 1972

Voodoo: Truth & Fantasy; Laënnec Hurbon; Thames & Hudson; 1995